Authors
Andrej Démuth
Slávka Démuthová
Adrián Slavkovský

SPECTRUM SLOVAKIA Series
Volume 30

Mathematics and Beauty.
An Attempt to Link the Cognitive and Philosophical-Spiritual Aspects of Beauty

VEDA PETER LANG

Bibliographic Information published by the Deutsche Nationalbibliothek
The Deutsche Nationalbibliothek lists this publication in the Deutsche Nationalbibliografie; detailed bibliographic data is available in the internet at http://dnb.d-nb.de.

Authors: Andrej Démuth[1], Slávka Démuthová[2], Adrián Slavkovský[3]

[1] Department of Theory of Law and Social Sciences, Faculty of Law, Comenius University, Bratislava, Slovakia
[2] Department of Psychology, Faculty of Arts and Sciences, University of Ss. Cyril and Methodius, Trnava, Slovakia
[3] Department of Philosophy, Center for Cognitive Studies, Faculty of Arts, Trnava University, Trnava, Slovakia

ISSN 2195-1845
ISBN 978-3-631-79488-3
Ebook: 978-3-631-79489-0
ePub: 978-3-631-79490-6
MOBI: 978-3-631-79491-3

ISBN 978-80-224-1764-8

Peter Lang – Berlin • Bern • Bruxelles • New York • Oxford • Warszawa • Wien

This publication has been peer reviewed.

www.peterlang.com www.veda.sav.sk

This work was supported by the Slovak Research and Development Agency under contract No. APVV-15-0294.

Contents

1. Introduction – Let None but the Geometric Enter Here

Andrej Démuth,
Slávka Démuthová,
Adrián Slavkovský

In his book *Úhelný kámen evropské vzdělanosti a moci* (*The Cornerstone of European Scholarship and Power*) (Vopěnka 2001, 53), Petr Vopěnka expressed his belief that it was not the desire for truth, but rather awe and beauty, which led ancient philosophers to an interest in theoretical knowledge. Knowledge would be acquired regardless, by the common utilization of objects or by word of mouth,[1] but an interest in knowledge for its own sake is what separates a barbaric approach to knowledge to that of the ancient philosophers. A barbarian (whatever interpretation of this word we choose to use) does not observe the world for the world itself. He is only interested in survival, in fulfilling his goals, desires and needs; and knowledge is only one of the means to achieve these ends. That is why he does not hesitate to use objects for purposes other than those which they were made for - he does not find it necessary to learn why a thing is as it is, how it is linked to its history, being, etc. The only relevant aspect of it is whether it meets his needs. Ancient thinkers, however, observed things for different reasons. They were interested in the things themselves, in their nature, laws, being. A pre-eminent example of this is the concept of theory, which is the centrepiece of the Greek understanding of the meaning and nature of knowledge.

The term *theory* means "viewing", "beholding". In his *On the Soul*, Aristotle adds that it always pertains to observation, speculation, but also contemplation - the highest form of philosophical activity (Aristotle 1996). However, theory is not an observation focused on finding a secondary purpose or personal gain. On the contrary, it is characterized by an interest in a thing for the thing itself. We study it not so we can better manipulate it or to achieve certain goals, but because the thing and its being interests us.[2] To be able to study it well, however, as Martin Heidegger (Heidegger 1995, 165) points out, we need sufficient time. Theoretical observations are therefore characterized by us having the time and desire to observe, view, behold, imagine, speculate and test things both hypothetically and in reality - to occupy ourselves with them, to get to know them better. The value of such activity dwells in the finding itself, not in any further use of it. That is what theory and the Greek notion of knowledge have in common with beauty.

---

1 Builders in ancient Mesopotamia and Egypt used strings in their work long before the birth of geometry and solved their daily tasks without any knowledge of theoretical laws.

2 Aristotle distinguishes between theory and *episteme* (understanding - De an, II 1: Met. VIII, 6., Phys. VII 3, EN VII 5). Knowing has a certain episteme and uses it - realizes it (I know because I know that...). In contrast, *techne* is a process of crafting, from the very beginning focused on the given goal - function.

For many philosophers, beauty does not have any individual function, except for occupying our minds and forcing us to perceive. The purpose of beautiful objects is to be, and if they were created as works of art, maybe also to be liked. Beauty is thus not something that would stop a barbarian. A barbarian does not recognize beauty. Specifically, he has no time for it. His worldview does not take it into account, similar to knowledge for the sake of knowledge.

One of the spaces where beauty meets knowledge is mathematics. In this book we will attempt to illustrate that what we find alluring in mathematics often has much in common with beauty, and, vice versa, that beauty is, as it were, a mathematical entity, or is often linked to mathematical operations, calculations and that its characteristic traits can be expressed through mathematical analysis. We will also try to show that just as mathematics is not an eminently theoretical discipline without any real impact on the world and our practical actions, so is beauty, though apparently entirely purposeless, not just a pleasant feeling, but that the perception of beauty is principally contaminated by epistemic content and has a deeper function than is obvious at first glance. The object of the following reflections will therefore not only be the relationship between mathematics and beauty (what makes mathematics attractive, what are the characteristics of mathematic beauty and what do mathematics and beauty have in common), but also to what extent can we analyse beauty mathematically and whether we carry out any calculations in perceiving beauty, what is the metaphysical status of mathematical and beautiful objects and so on.

2. Mathematics as Seeking Symmetry

Mathematics is among the oldest disciplines of human knowledge and has developed independently everywhere where there is evidence of human culture.[3] It not only includes simple calculations, but also the investigation of the laws of quantity, structure, space and change and in its observations leans on both visual thinking (geometry) and abstract thinking. Mathematicians (gr. μαθηματικός (*mathematikós*) from μάθημα (*máthēma*), "knowledge") - scholars - were thus people who not only knew something, but (according to Aristotle's claim from the *Posterior Analytics*) also knew the "why". Their knowledge did not come purely from a need for solutions to real issues, but from the results of theoretical exercises and a purely theoretical interest in the object of observation and the relationships between individual objects. That may be the reason why ancient scholars often eventually found the objects they were interested in outside of the common material world. Pythagoreans understood numbers as divine entities and did not see geometric objects as bound to the inventory of the material-burdened world. A geometrical triangle is not one that you trace with a finger in the sand, nor is it the one carved in stone. The triangle of which we can speak is the one in the ideal - geometrical world. The worlds of geometry and algebra cannot be plumbed by one's own eyes. The line you can see is never perfectly straight, infinite and single-dimensional. What you perceive is just a material, imperfect simulacrum. "True" geometrically straight lines only exist in the world of ideas.

No surprise then, that Platonic philosophy is so well received among mathematicians. Its essence is the world of ideas. Truth, if it is to be, in fact, true, needs to apply to something eternal, infinite, immutable, something that can be known without fear that in a few moments that knowledge will no longer be true (Démuth 2013b). That is something the material world simply cannot offer. Entering the world of truths is therefore entering the spaces "beyond the world"[4] - it is the art of finding the signs and archetypes of something eternal and divine in this world - of something, which

3 It is interesting that in various epochs and geographic areas, mathematics developed independently and uniquely. The history of European mathematics often overlooks the relatively well-developed Indian system, which included a positioning system, zero, the decimal system and the rich use of fractions and exponents. In Mesopotamia, a multitude of tablets can be found that document the use of natural numbers and positive sexagesimal fractions, but also problems suggesting linear, quadratic, cubic and biquadratic equations, as well as practicing problems that lead to octic equations. Chinese mathematics also developed independently of European and, using rod calculus, solved problems similar to the Indian ones using different methods. Similarly, the Chinese discovered the Pythagorean theorem in a different way.

4 Not in vain did the Greek gods dwell on Olympus - a mountain the summit of which is obscured by clouds, and their truths are therefore hidden from mortal sight.

is true. The ability to see the eternal contents is not always entirely natural and innate. It is often the case that a person needs to be initiated to allow them to see otherworldly objects.[5]

One of the classical examples of the initiation of a candidate to knowledge of science is education. As Petr Vopěnka (Vopěnka 2001, 34) suggests, teaching mathematics is about demonstrating facts and their evidence. A teacher can only demonstrate using examples, by means of which he reveals the given knowledge, but the pupil must see the knowledge by himself in the examples. It is therefore not irrelevant which roads are taken to knowledge, which roads do our thoughts travel. Sometimes, in demonstrating the mathematical world, the road of thought itself - the method of thinking - is beautiful, because by understanding it the pupil attains a tool that can reveal other - new (hitherto unknown) content. On such a road, one may encounter many remarkable, unexpected and alluring objects, or not - the road only being a tedious sequence of necessary steps. Sometimes, there are multiple roads to the result,[6] and the choice of some of them may be more confusing than enlightening for a candidate. In such cases, a student does not perceive the laws, nor does he fully understand how he got to where he is and what it is that he perceives. He is but the silent witness to a spectacle he does not comprehend. If a candidate does not see the revelation of truth, he only perceives the demonstrated examples and does not understand. In contrast, if he understands why, the route his mind must follow and where his teacher is taking him, he will understand not only the laws and the beauty of the road, but will also see the ideas revealed in their own world and understand them. The Evidence of these relationships is often clear and self-evident and therefore do not need any further proof.[7] Some basic proofs are entirely natural and do not need any hints. Some only appear after we are shown, or after the road we need to take to see them is suggested to us.

---

5 Adrián Slavkovský differentiates between the beauty of method, the beauty of result and the beauty of mathematical experience. The issue of being initiated into the process of perceiving the beauty of mathematics is the issue of the beauty of method (methodos - walking down a road). Its object is the formulation of a problem, the road of discovery itself and the prospective beauty of proof (Slavkovský 2017, 145–147).

6 For example, the American mathematician Elicha Scott Loomis (Loomis 1968) collected and published 367 different methods of proving the Pythagorean theorem.

7 It is remarkable that the Greeks perceived numbers as geometric shapes, and many of their proofs were based on evidence and opinion, i.e. on seeing. From this also sprang our visual metaphors for the proof, clarification, demonstration and evidence. One of the most remarkable self-evident geometric proofs is the validity of the equation $(a+b)^2=a^2+2ab+b^2$ by means of a square, the side of which has a length of (a+b). By drawing it properly, the initiate directly evidences that its area comprises a square with a side a, a square with a side b and two rectangles with sides a and b.

2.1. Trivial and Non-trivial Proofs

Classical trivial proofs were known to the Greeks even before Pythagoreans. Pythagoreans, however, looked deeper and saw relations and proportions which eluded the un-initiated. Not only the relations and proportions, but also the numbers that express them. "These proportions were, on one hand, studied in general and on the other hand, there was the search for various highly specific proportions for the sizes of geometrical objects. Of these, such as the proportions of the diagonal and sides of a square, various pieces of knowledge were collected. The crowning finding was the expression of a specific proportion by a numerical ratio" (Vopěnka 2001, 53).

Findings that are numbers can be considered a finding of the pronounceability of the beauty of the result. To wit, some results are beautiful in themselves, whether by their compactness, or, vice versa, by the fact they cannot be grasped and their immeasurable appeal.[8] Pythagoreans very quickly understood that the number one is the smallest possible number. Its potential division into smaller parts does not lessen it, but rather moves the whole to a lower level (a part becomes a whole). It is therefore evident that the number one is the foundation of everything and, in principle, is indivisible and divine. Without its existence, no other number or value would be possible. An analogy for the number one in geometry is a point[9] and in physics, for a long time, it was the Democritean atom.[10] Pythagoreans approached other numbers in the same way: "two symbolized the dimorphic female principle, graphically represented by a line segment. "Only the connection of the female and the divine created the first real number, three. It characterized the male principle and expressed a plane in geometry, but also a beginning, middle and end, soul, matter and three-dimensionality" (Karamanides 2006, 63). Magic and mysticism accompanies the entire Pythagorean understanding of numbers: the number four as the first spatial object - the tetrahedron as a symbol of order, six as a symbol of perfection and fullness - it contains its divisors, and similarly the number ten, which contains the sacred tetractys (1+2+3+4); but among these Pythagoreans found relations which changed our approach to knowledge from the mythical to the scientific. This can be best illustrated by the symbol of Pythagoreanism - the pentagram" (Démuth 2013b).

8 For example, periodic or infinite non-periodic numbers, etc.
9 A point as that which does not have dimensions (Euclid).
10 The atom as the indivisible basic building block of nature.

The pentagram - a five-pointed star inscribed in a pentagon in such a way that it connects all its vertices - even today is a symbol of many mystical references and occult movements. As will soon be clear, this is because it hides a multiplicity of interesting relations. It is regular and equilateral. A regular pentagon not only has five equal sides, but these also form five equal interior angles. At the same time, its diagonals form a pentagram, in the centre of which a new, albeit smaller, inverted pentagon is located. By connecting the diagonals of this smaller one, a new inverted pentagon can be formed, and so on, ad infinitum.

The self-similarity (the attribute of a shape that has the same characteristic structure independent of angle, scale or the resolution of the perceiver) and self-replicability of a pentagon are indisputably noteworthy attributes. It is these, together with relatively simple rules of recursion, that form the basis of fractals, as studied in fractal geometry.

Another particularity of the self-similarity of regular pentagons formed by the intersections of their diagonals is their ratios. Each of the embedded pentagons is related to the size of the original pentagon by the golden ratio in such a progression. The golden ratio is a specific ratio that expresses the division of a segment of line into two unequal parts in such a way that the ratio of the two parts is the same as the ratio of the larger of the parts to the whole. At first glance, there is nothing exceptional in case of this ratio. Empirical research, however, suggests that this ratio of dividing any two parts to a whole is considered to be the most aesthetically pleasing. Maybe that is the reason why Pythagoreans labelled such a ratio and the number that expresses it as golden. However, here dwell other secrets of the pentagon.

This recurrence coming from the law of the golden ratio means that the diagonal of a regular pentagon divides another of the diagonals in a golden ratio. This succession of the formation of nested pentagons also shows that the diagonal and side of such pentagon are incommensurable. This means that the ratio of their lengths cannot be expressed by the ratio of any two integers. For Pythagoreanism, believing that all the relations in the world can be expressed numerically, this fact was absolutely devastating. Numbers that cannot be expressed as a ratio of two integers (i.e. as fractions, or rational numbers) are irrational. And irrationality, as Mario Livio (Livio 2002, 39) shows, is unbearable for rational beings.

The essence of irrational numbers is that they cannot be expressed by rational numbers. The square root of two, which calculates the diagonal of a square with a side with a length of one, would have to be expressed as a fraction $\sqrt{2}=(a/b)$, which has no common divisor in the numerator and denominator. That means that the numerator and denominator cannot be even numbers (a common divisor would be the number two). At the same time, the denominator cannot be an even number (the numerator must be even, as the square of an even number is always even ($a^2=2b^2$)). The denominator therefore can only be an odd number, because the square of an odd number is always odd, but, at the same time, since it is another number multiplied by two ($a^2=2b^2$), it must be even (as any number multiplied by two is always even), and that is a logical contradiction. The square root of any number, which is not the square of an integer, is therefore always an irrational number.

Furthermore, as was later discovered, the golden ratio also expresses the ratio of any two consecutive terms in the Fibonacci sequence. The Fibonacci sequence is a sequence of numbers in which every term F, after the first two, in the sequence, is the sum of the previous two terms. For example, 1, 1, 2, 3, 5, 8, 13, 21, 34, 55, 89, 144, 233, 377, 610, 987, 1597, 2584, 4181, 6765, 10946, 17711, 28657, 46368, 75025, 121393, etc. Johannes Kepler had already pointed out that the division of any two consecutive Fibonacci sequence numbers $F(n+1)/F(n)$ converges to φ, which is used to denote the golden ratio.

Eventually, Kepler's ideas led him to the admiration of Platonic regular solids. He knew that a regular dodecahedron can be constructed from regular pentagons, which is similar to a sphere, and which could therefore be inscribed into a circular orbit around one of the known celestial bodies. In his *Mysterium Cosmographicum* (with the subtitle *Forerunner of the Cosmological Essays, Which Contains the Secret of the Universe; on the Marvelous Proportion of the Celestial Spheres, and on the True and Particular Causes of the Number, Magnitude, and Periodic Motions of the Heavens; Established by Means of the Five Regular Geometric Solids)* (Latin: *Prodromus dissertationum cosmographicarum, continens mysterium cosmographicum, de admirabili proportione orbium coelestium, de que causis coelorum numeri, magnitudinis, motuumque periodicorum genuinis & proprijs, demonstratum, per quinque regularia corpora geometrica),* he postulated the positions and distances of Mercury, Venus, Earth, Mars, Jupiter and Saturn on the basis of geometrical principles nested in the orbits inscribed in the Platonic solids: octahedron, icosahedron, dodecahedron, tetrahedron, cube. And though Kepler later dismissed his astronomical formulations because they were not precise enough, it was the finding of the "divine proportions", orderliness and system of the world - universe and nature - which fascinated him the most in mathematics and astronomy.

Therefore, Pythagoreans and other mathematicians not only found a mathematically expressible principle of what is aesthetically pleasing to us in the golden ratio, but, and more pointedly, also rational principles and systems (or world and universe, but also simple mathematical relations and laws), which we consider important and interesting. Furthermore, these findings are not given to us directly; we have to gradually reveal them and for that, we are rewarded by their beauty.[11]

Multiple mathematicians therefore talk about the charm and mystery of mathematics and numbers. When answering why numbers are beautiful, Hungarian mathematician Paul Erdős states, in a way almost typical of a Pythagorean: "It's like asking why Beethoven's Ninth Symphony is beautiful. If you don't see why, someone can't tell you. I know numbers are beautiful. If they aren't beautiful, nothing is" (Devlin 2000, 140). Similarly, Bertrand Russell perceives the beauty of mathematics in itself "Mathematics, rightly viewed, possesses not only truth, but supreme beauty - a beauty cold and austere, like that of sculpture, without appeal to any part of our weaker nature, without the gorgeous trappings of paintings or music, yet sublimely pure, and capable of a stern perfection such as only the greatest art can show. The true spirit of delight, the exaltation, the sense of being more than Man, which is the touchstone of the highest excellence, is to be found in mathematics as surely as in poetry" (Russell 1917, 60).

What is it then that makes mathematics beautiful and attractive? It seems to be its logic and orderliness. Maryam Mirzakani, the first woman to be awarded the Fields Medal, recounts: "My first memory of mathematics is probably the time [my brother] told me about the problem of adding numbers from 1 to 100". This was the story of Carl Gauss, the 18th-century genius whose schoolteacher set him this problem as a timewasting exercise - only for his precocious pupil to calculate the answer in a matter of seconds. The obvious solution is simple but slow: 1+2+3+4. Gauss's solution is quicker to execute, and far more cunning. It goes like this: Divide the numbers into two groups - from 1 to 50, and from 51 to 100. Then, add them together in pairs, starting with the lowest (1) and the highest (100), and working inwards (2+99, 3+98 and so on). There are 50 pairs; the sum of each pair is 101; the answer is 5050. "That was the first time I enjoyed a beautiful solution", Mirzakhani told the Clay Mathematics Institute in 2008 (Flyn 2017). Many other mathematicians and geniuses feel the same way. That which entices them is the search for elegance, orderliness and logic in simple, but also highly complex problems and solutions.[12]

11 That is why, Vopěnka hints at his disdain for those who ostentatiously exhibit the secret of the pentagon without knowing its basis.

12 In this regard, the famous mathematician G. H. Hardy stated: "The mathematician's patterns, like the painter's or the poet's must be *beautiful*; the ideas, like the colours or the words, must fit together in a harmonious way. Beauty is the first test: there is no permanent place in the world for ugly mathematics" (Hardy 1940, 14).

In 2016 "BBC Earth asked mathematicians and physicists to tell us which equations they think are the most beautiful. Their choices ranged from explanations of antimatter to the prediction of how sub-atomic particles behave" (Hogenboom 2016). Among the most appreciated were: the Dirac equation, Riemann's formula, Pi, the Euler-Lagrange equation, the Yang-Baxter equation, Euler's identity, Bayes's theorem, the wave equation, Einstein's field equation, the logistic map, a "simple" arithmetic progression, Hamilton's quaternion formula, but another selection also included Pythagoras's theorem, Newton's equation and Einstein's equations for the special theory of relativity. The essence of the beauty of all these equations and findings is that they express exceedingly complex relations in relatively large fields of study in a relatively simple and elegant manner. The number pi can be used as an example.

Archimedes' constant or Ludolphian numbers[13] are defined as $\varpi=c/d$ (the ratio of a circle's circumference to its diameter), but also as the ratio of the area of a circle to the square of its radius[14] ($\varpi=S/r^2$). At the same time, ϖ is an exceedingly important number, with which we can explain the geometry of the world and carry out geometric constructions. Similarly, possibly the most famous equation in physics, Einstein's mass-energy equivalence, expresses that anything with mass has an equivalent amount of energy and vice versa (E can be calculated as the mass (m) multiplied by the speed of light (c) squared).

David Stipp wrote a book titled *A Most Elegant Equation: Euler's Formula and the Beauty of Mathematics* in 2017, in which he describes one of the most remarkable equations in the history of mathematics. Euler's identity or Euler's equation is the basic formula of complex analysis, expressing the relationship between five mathematical constants (1 – the basis of all other numbers, 0 – the concept of nothingness, pi – the number that defines a circle, e – the number that underlies exponential growth, i – the "imaginary" square root of -1) and three of the basic arithmetic operations (addition, multiplication and exponentiation) which all occur exactly once each. That is why it is sometimes referred to as the divine equation.

These equations have not only the formal simplicity and epistemically

---

13 According to the German-Dutch mathematician Ludolph van Ceulen.

14 It's an obvious paradox that the surface area of a circle is calculated via the surface area of a square ("ϖr squared", even though they are usually round). That led to the creation of the problem of correlation of a circle and a square (or, of a sphere and a cube) – a grave issue proposed by ancient geometers. It is also known as a problem of constructing a square having the equivalent are as a set circle, using only a compass and a ruler. The (squaring the circle) task was proven as impossible through Lindemann-Weierstrass theorem in 1882.

valuable ability to reveal the order and relations between objects in common, but also in the way they achieve this. It seems they do so by means of unusual symmetries. It is the balances and symmetries that are the basic building blocks of both beauty and knowledge.

2.2. Symmetry

The etymology of the Greek term "symmetry" tends to be derived from the Ancient Greek *σύμμετρος* - *sym* (with) and *metron* (measure) and expresses "the relation of parts, proportion", in Middle French *symmétrie* (16c.) and directly from Latin *symmetria*, from Greek *symmetria* "agreement of dimensions, due proportion, arrangement", from *symmetros* "having a common measure, even, proportionate", from the assimilated form of *syn-* "together" (see syn-) + *metron* "measure" (from PIE root *me- (2) "to measure"). Meaning "harmonic arrangement of parts" (Harper 2018b) and refers to the commensurability, i.e. the ability to find a common unit of measurement when evaluating an object. Any two things are incommensurable if there is no common element or aspect which could be used to compare them. If things or their parts have nothing in common, it is impossible to reflect upon or discuss them.[15] On the contrary, thinking allows us to understand what is organized and governed by a common rule. We are normally capable of understanding parts of a whole because they are organized internally in such a way that it is clear they belong to the same unit, and they are organized in this unit based on certain rules. The discovery of these rules is then art conditioned by an intellectual (for instance, mathematical) operation.

Symmetry is thus not a uniform reflection. It means to find a specific type of organization. In mathematics, it is expressed by geometrical or arithmetical arrangements dependent on certain rules or criterion.[16]

15 According to Aristotle, science may only focus on what individuals have in common, not on the unique characteristics of individuality, but only its general aspects. It is not possible to create a science of the unique characteristics of individuality, or of the individuality of an individual.

16 The most common geometric symmetries are: reflection symmetry, line symmetry, mirror symmetry, mirror-image symmetry - symmetry with respect to reflection, rotational symmetry (rotation about a fixed point without changing the overall shape), translational symmetry, helical symmetry, scale symmetry, glide reflection symmetry and roto-reflective symmetry. Mathematics finds symmetry in calculations, symmetric probability distributions and in many other areas.

(Mathematical symmetry may be observed with respect to the passage of time; as a spatial relationship; through geometric transformations; through other kinds of functional transformations; and as an aspect of abstract objects, theoretical models, language, music and even knowledge itself - Mainzer 2005, Kisak 2016). In logic, it refers to the identical nature of certain properties (such as equivalence or logical biconditional). In chemistry, symmetry is a property of the relationships and interactions between molecules; it enables us to understand the dipole moment, spectroscopic transitions or crystal structures and, for example, their optical properties. It is a fundamental physical property since it represents a certain type of invariance. The laws of physics may be understood as specific manifestations of symmetry. They include, for instance, the symmetry of forces or fields, various local or global symmetries (e.g. the symmetry of space-time), diverse types of continuous symmetry, discrete symmetries or even supersymmetries. They even apply to the most minute, microscopic levels of space, as well as to the subtlest levels of the micro-cosmos - in the field of elementary particles. As proven by the German mathematician Emma Noether, symmetry is responsible, for shifts in time through the laws of energy conservation, for shifts in space through the law of the conservation of linear momentum and through rotational symmetry for the conservation of angular momentum. For this reason, physicians believe that the essential characteristics of nature are symmetrical. In our "mirrored world", particles are counterbalanced by antiparticles, positive forces by negative, attraction by repulsion, action by reaction, energy by mass and speed. The laws of the conservation and transformation of energy apply here. In 2008, Yoichiro Nambu was awarded the Nobel Prize for Physics "for the discovery of the mechanism of spontaneous broken symmetry in subatomic physics" (Nambu 2018), he showed that the original fundamental symmetry in the physics of solid substances is disrupted at a subatomic level, resulting in the phenomenon whereby certain substances have something other than a neutral expression (e.g. the resulting magnetization of a substance is orientated to a specific direction from an infinite number of initially equal options). Alongside Nambu, Makoto Kobayashi and Toshihide Maskawa were also awarded the Nobel Prize for Physics "for the discovery of the origin of the broken symmetry which predicts the existence of at least three families of quarks in nature" (Kobayashi 2018, Maskawa 2018). The discovery of these local disturbances of the original global symmetry of elementary particles is the basic tool for the explanation of symmetries in quantum mechanics which describe the features of space-time and the particles that are left unchanged in certain transformations, using quantum mechanics, relativist quantum mechanics (symmetries in general relativity) and quantum field theory, applying mathematical formulations of the standard model and physics of condensed matter. Yet it is obvious that the main methodological tool for the exploration and explanation of the aforementioned symmetries and their possible divergences is mathematics and mathematical thinking (often group theories).

In biology, symmetry expresses the fundamental properties of most organisms. That it is possible to identify more asymmetries than symmetries from observations of most organisms is quite remarkable. Our "front" has a substantially different shape to our "back", the upper part of the body differs from the "bottom" and "the inside" is completely different to the "outside". Most organisms capable of linear movement are only symmetrical in the direction of their prevailing motion. Gradual evolution and specialization have resulted in us having a different morphological structure, differentiating the front of the body from the back (the eyes are in the front, aimed in the direction of movement, just like most receptors and limbs) and the upper from the lower. Bilateral animals are more or less symmetrical with respect to the sagittal or longitudinal plane which divides the body into left and right halves.[17] Other organisms such as sea anemones often have radial or rotational symmetry, since their movement is unpredictable. But strangely, the stem cells from which the given symmetrical or asymmetrical organism evolved are, in principle, symmetrical.[18] The whole of our existence starts from a relatively simple and relatively symmetrical cell - the zygote, which has the potential to create all the cells that constitute us and that will ever constitute us. This initially symmetrical cell splits into two symmetrical cells - completely identical copies of itself. Even this step results in a disruption of the basic symmetry, as the initial zygote divides by cleavage and the new two-cell formation is only axially symmetrical. These newly formed cells divide in the same way,

17 "A major division of the animal kingdom comprising all forms with a bilaterally symmetrical body plan (that is, their left and right sides are mirror images, or nearly so) and organ systems that develop from three tissue layers. The animal kingdom, Metazoa, is subdivided into about 30 major animal groups, or phyla, each constructed on a different architectural plan. Most of these phyla are grouped as the Bilateria, comprising a major early branch on the family tree of animals that may have originated nearly 600 million years ago. All bilaterians possess some features that are not perfectly symmetrical (e.g., the human heart and liver), but all have descended from an essentially bilateral ancestor" (Valentine 2014).

18 We are referring to the first cell - the zygote - which is formed after two sexually differentiated cells, gametes, join. The zygote is relatively perfectly symmetrical, even though one of the gametes (sperm) is only axially symmetrical due to its need for forward motion.

until they create a sphere-shaped cluster of identical, ontogenetically non-specific (no skin, neuron, skeleton or muscle cells) cells - the morula. The zygote, just as the cells of morula, is totipotent, which means that under appropriate conditions a process of differentiation can create any cell in the body. The original axial symmetry of the initial division of the zygote then changes into the multi-axial symmetry of the identical non-specific cells of the morula. So, where does the specification and symmetrical disturbance of stem cells come from? It seems obvious that it starts somewhere during this process or in its continuation (the division of the morula into the blastula, which divides further into the gastrula, based on the genetic information in these cells). It is in this process where asymmetry allows the cells to split into various structures that fulfil different functions in the organism. Scientists at the Francis Crick Institute working at the Polarity and Patterning Networks Laboratory understand that the explanation is hidden in the information found within the double-helix spiral discovered by the founder of the Institute. After discovering DNA, Crick and Watson understood that through four basic nitrogenous bases (adenine (A), guanine (G), cytosine (C) and thymine (T)), their combination, repetition and transcription, it is possible to compose virtually any "composition" that results in the organic "composition - structure" of the body. The "only" problem is to understand the patterns and to unveil the invisible codes in order for us to understand them[19]. And it is the understanding and clarification of the rules of how and why the differentiation of our cells takes place in the process of ontogenesis that is the subject of intense interest and research at this biomedical institute.

Symmetry disruption is the first step to creating polarization, individualization and identification. It orientates cells with their specific direction. Polarization makes cells distinguish one side from the other, which subsequently enables them to divide and create two separate cells. It is only through this process or its results which makes us individual and enables us to have the distinctive features that make us different (for ourselves and others) to others - which ultimately makes us ourselves.

Therefore, several scientists note that there is no such thing as perfect or complete symmetry in the realm of real existence. Not only because no two cells, objects or formations are never completely identical (they do

19 In this sense, Sarah Howe composed a poem entitled *New Music*, which only uses four letters (just as several musical composers compose their pieces only using the tones B, A, C, H in honour of J. S. Bach), which together with the song by Chu-li Shewring entitled *"New Music: Making sense of the Noise"*, documents the indefinite variability of endless instructions.

not share, for example, the same time and space of occurrence), but also because there is no such thing as a perfectly mirrored image.[20] Commensurability, symmetry or similarity of objects is not necessarily that they are completely and absolutely identical, but only their mutual similarity or the similarity of their relations.[21] Perhaps this is what the Polish poet Julian Tuwim had in mind when he referred to symmetry as the aesthetics of idiots. Complete symmetry often does not exist, and if it did, it would be utterly boring. As stated by Alan Lightman in reference to Ernst Gombrich "If everything is perfectly symmetric, and this is including a work of art, we find it boring. ... On the other hand, if everything is random, with no symmetry at all, we're confused. And so you want to sort of navigate between boredom on the one hand and confusion on the other". Therefore, he claims that beauty lies instead in "symmetry, with a little asymmetry mixed in" (Hockenberry, Spiropulu, Lightman, Gross, Dijkgraaf 2016). True attractiveness then lies in the slightly disturbed symmetry of an object.[22]

2.2.1. The Attractiveness of Symmetry

From where comes the enormous attractiveness and epistemic priority of symmetry, if most of the objects in the world are not symmetrical but

20 In order to explain this phenomenon in Leibniz's logic and metaphysics, we apply the principle of indiscernibleness (*identitas indiscernibilium*), which postulates that if two individual substances have indiscernible qualities, they are not two substances, but only a single substance - they are identical. Each two individual substances have to differ from each other, even if only by a single discernible property, such as spatiotemporal locality.

21 Thus, symmetry does not express the complete identity, but rather the identity of two or more relations in different situations.

22 The reason why perfect symmetry bores and does not interest for long lies in the complete compression of knowledge. There is nothing more to learn in a field where we have already revealed all the rules of arrangement and complexity. The appealing must diverge from this revealed organization. This is why the history of fashion and art includes movements which programmatically employ the distortion of symmetry in their systems. This is the case for the Baroque beauty mark (fluctuating asymmetry), which was supposed to distort the symmetry of the face or draw attention to itself and by doing so divert attention from other - natural asymmetries. Similarly, Art Nouveau introduced mostly natural ornaments to art, the role of which was to distort the symmetry of ornaments and by doing so increase the complexity of the evaluated object by searching for higher rules of organization. Japanese aesthetics even include an entire concept of imperfection and asymmetry (wabi sabi), which expresses the need for further improvement through the acknowledgement of imperfection. Temples built in this cannon contained aspects of architectural imperfection (e.g. inverted pillar) or unfinished work (room), so that the temple or palace could be further developed. Disruption of symmetries is, therefore, intellectually interesting, as it forces the search for higher levels of organization.

mostly asymmetrical and complete symmetry is not so common in nature? In their study *Symmetry, beauty and evolution* (Enquist, Arak 1994), Magnus Enquist and Anthony Arak assert that people, as well as several other animal species, react very sensitively to symmetrical patterns and prefer them in comparison to asymmetrical or disorganized patterns. Such behaviour is normally explained through biologically determined responses to impulses as well as through the reduced energy burden in identifying symmetry in so-called exploratory behaviour. It is also assumed that a certain level of symmetry signals a certain quality of the signaller, hence our preference for symmetrical objects. However, Enquist and Arak imply that "the existence of a sensory bias for symmetry may have been exploited independently by natural selection acting on biological signals and through human artistic innovation. This may account for the observed convergence to symmetrical forms in nature and decorative art... Preferences for symmetry may arise as a by-product of the need to recognize objects irrespective of their position and orientation in the visual field" (Enquist, Arak 1994, 169). Our sensory apparatus was formed through evolution to provide the maximum ability to discern objects in the area where the fields of perception of both paired organs overlap. This means that we are able to perceive signals most sensitively and clearly in the area where the fields of perceptions of the pair of individually functioning sensory apparatus overlap (e.g. the right and left eyes, right and left ears). In general, signals best stimulate the sensory apparatus when they are perceived well in all possible positions and directions (Enquist, Arak 1994, 171). It is mostly symmetrical objects which fulfil this requirement, particularly due to the overlap of the paired receptor organs (possible deficiencies in the perception of one receptor are compensated for by the other). This study equally assumes that the preference for symmetrical patterns observed in most animal species may be related to the way that these receptors are connected to the nerve cells in the brain. One way or another, symmetrical patterns are apparently more easily detected in our environment, and we prefer them because they fulfil an important informational purpose for us.

In the video entitled *Beyond Beauty: The predictive power of symmetry,*[23] John Heckenberry states that one of the most striking benefits of the perception of symmetry is its predictive potential. When we see the right half

23 The video below is a panel discussion (the World Science Festival in New York City, NYU Skirball Center: 4 June 2016) by the mathematician Robbert Dijkgraaf, writer Alan Lightman, physician Maria Spiropulu and the Nobel Prize Laureate for Physics David Gross (Hockenberry, Spiropulu, Lightman, Gross, Dijkgraaf 2016).

of someone's face, based on our previous experience and the data we perceive from this half, we can quite accurately estimate what the other, so far unseen, half is most probably going to look like. Naturally, our estimate may be incorrect or inaccurate, but we would be truly surprised if it was completely wrong. The reason is that faces occur in nature as relatively symmetrical objects, and we presume that the perceived face will be as such too. Furthermore, this strategy - to anticipate a mirror or almost mirror image of the other half of the face - is the most convenient in terms of energy. Logically we know that a presumption of the form of non-perceived reality based on the perceived reality is not entirely justified. In the theory of possible worlds, there is an infinite number of possibilities for how the other (not perceived) half of the face might look. So why prefer its mirror image? The reason may be that it is extremely energy-consuming to work with many potential scenarios,[24] and we therefore choose the one which seems to be the most plausible on the basis of the perceived data. But where does this plausibility stem from?

In this sense, Alan Lightman points out that the nature only makes use of the most energy-efficient solutions. He gave the example of the bee honeycomb. It has the shape of a perfectly regular hexagon. There are only three types of regular shapes which can be placed next to each other without any gaps in between - the equilateral triangle, the square and the equilateral hexagon. However, the advantage of the hexagon is that it has the same surface area while having the shortest perimeter.[25] This way, bees do not waste energy in the construction of the honeycomb (it needs the least amount of wax), and the unused energy can be used for their nutrition. The same principle is in operation when we predict the other half of a face. Making use of the existing knowledge and flipping it on a mirror plane is the most energy-efficient method of prediction. More convenient than tiresomely forming something new on a completely new basis. Similarly, a sixth of a snowflake (or even a half of a sixth) allows us to easily reconstruct the shape of the whole snowflake with a great degree of accuracy

24 In this case, it is the amount, which is only limited by our imagination.

25 In around 300 A.D., Pappus of Alexandria presented the idea that the hexagon is the geometric shape with the shortest perimeter, capable of covering a plane without any excess. However, he could not justify his reasoning mathematically. The justification came around 1700 years later, in 1999, when Thomas Hales proved that Pappes was right. Similarly, Lord Kelvin presumed that the truncated octahedron is the three-dimensional object with a similar property (capable of filling an entire space without any excess and having the smallest surface area possible), until around 100 years later when Wearie and Phelan discovered the so-called Weaire-Phelan structure.

and with expenditure of the minimum amount of energy. Furthermore, employing a strategy of the principle of reflection carries one more significant advantage connected with the principle of the lowest energy usage.

Things that occur in the nature need to have a shape and a structure which will allow them to resist counteracting pressures and energies as efficiently as possible. Primarily, this facilitates the preservation of their stability. Planets are spherical because gravity formed them this way, and the spherical shape of soap bubble minimizes the surface pressure of the external environment. This also applies to the distribution of pressures and forces from snowflakes, through honeycombs, to the complex architecture of medieval cathedrals.

Experience has taught us that the existence of every action causes a symmetrical pressure on the existence of an equally strong counteracting reaction. This not only concerns physical forces, but also economic and social interactions (direct and indirect reciprocity). Thus, in order to preserve a certain stability, it is perhaps natural to anticipate and mirror the perceived images and balance of fundamental physical forces and effects. Even though a perfectly symmetrical face will never exist for various reasons. What is more, if the perceived face truly had perfectly symmetrical halves and the left half had been the perfect mirror image of the right half, the face would be symmetrical and beautiful, but at the same time, it would not look credible. Our experience teaches us that the world is not homogeneous and neither it is perfectly symmetrical, individual parts (due to the adoption of different positions in space) are not exposed to completely identical energies and pressures, which forces them to resist their effects differently.[26] Whether we realize it or not, each of us has a dominant eye, a dominant ear, etc.; and so we also have lateral preferences in our perception of the world. Accordingly, when looking at a human face, some people prefer to look at the right half while others prefer the left half depending on which eye and which half of the field of view is dominant for the particular individual. Yet, we expect a certain degree of organization and symmetry in the world. Not perfect perhaps, but at least good enough to allow us to consider organization and rules. Only as a result of this organization and rules are we able to navigate ourselves in the world, anticipate things and feel safer. We would feel quite lost, if we did not observe these rules.

Lateral facial symmetries allow doctors to assess whether a person is

---

26 For example, the intensity and direction of the arriving solar irradiance results in a different degree of tanning on either side of the face.

healthy, while axial and fluctuating asymmetries are symptoms of an illness or possible issues. An unusually positioned corner of the mouth or eye size maybe a symptom of a stroke, lesions or tumours, just as asymmetrical motor skills and other non-lateral expressions indicate unnatural states of health. In this sense, symmetry can be an indicator of health and hence, as shown by the numerous evolutionary interpretations, it plays a crucial part in mate selection. It turns out that women, as well as the females of other species, prefer their mates to have symmetrical features, which is related to a prediction of traits as well as evolutionary stability.

Positive correlations between attractiveness and facial or body symmetry tend to be interpreted using game theory and the prediction of desirable and stable genome properties of the individual. Facial symmetry anomalies are considered to be an expression of genes that indicate an elevated risk of potential genetic disorders or handicaps. So average faces appear to be the most attractive since they show none of the possible anomalies, and the average is interpreted as a form of symmetry. We perceive fluctuating symmetries in a similar way; they can often indicate random stress-induced deviations from perfect symmetry and reflect the ability of the individual to cope with a wide range of environmental stresses (e.g. Johnstone 1994). Examples of such fluctuating asymmetries include scars, wounds and asymmetries due to fractures, i.e. factors that predict an increased likelihood of violent or other types of risky behaviour. Even when the preference for male symmetry is the by-product of the selection for mate recognition (Johnstone 1994). As shown in the study of David Hope et al. (2013) facial symmetry indicates not only good health, but it also positively correlates with a higher socio-economic status and vice versa. A higher socio-economic status in youth was reflected in a higher degree of facial symmetry in relatively old people (83 years old) and vice versa, less symmetrical faces were associated with a lower socio-economic status in their youth. It seems, therefore, that disturbed symmetry provides a convenient indication of early-onset disorders (related to nutritional factors, high-risk behaviour, socio-economic reasons - e.g. lookism), while this predictor is not so transparent in the case of bodily symmetry. Whatever its cause, symmetry is, despite being relatively odd, such a crucial predictor and criterion that we have become extremely sensitive to it, we prefer it and associate it with different values (important for us), one of which is undoubtedly beauty.[27]

27 "The pleasures of the senses which most closely approach the pleasures of the mind, and are the most pure and certain, are those of music and symmetry, the former [being pleasure] of the ears, the latter of the eyes; for it is easy to understand the principles [raisons] of

2.2.2. Symmetry in Mathematics

As previously mentioned, symmetry belongs among the core attributes of imaging and depiction. Its essence is that the given object corresponds to itself based on some symmetric operation (rotation, folding, shift, etc.). The Ancient Greeks were aware of these basic symmetries - central (point), axial and planar. That is why in their treatises, they preferred those geometric shapes and trajectories which were symmetric (circle, sphere, equilateral triangle, etc.), and considered them to be perfect. This preference for evident symmetries certainly has its upsides and can be found all around us - in architecture, art and nature (the wings of butterflies, flower petals, shapes of leaves, snowflakes, bee combs, crystals, minerals and gems). To be enthralled by perfectly symmetrical objects is understandable and in Pythagoreanism, Renaissance and even today, a large proportion of (mostly the evolutionarily and psychologically focused) the studies of beauty deal with various types of symmetry of the body, face, etc. Perfect symmetry in objects is genuinely rare and, due to this quality, it arouses unusual attention. As a multitude of evolutionary and bio-psychological studies suggest, however, bodily and facial symmetry has an important informative value, pointing to the facts hidden underneath (gene expression).

In geometry, symmetries are found more often than in nature. All regular polygons show axial symmetry, with the number of axes of symmetry corresponding to the number of vertices of a given polygon. For example, an isosceles triangle has a single axis of symmetry, an equilateral triangle has three, a square four, a regular hexagon six. A circle or disk has an infinite number of such axes - lines passing through the centre of the circle. Similarly, a sphere, cube, rectangular cuboid and other regular objects have at least one axis of symmetry. Some of them also show planar symmetry (e.g. a cube has nine planes of symmetry, a rectangular cuboid has three), and some are centrally symmetrical (cube, sphere, cylinder, etc.). No surprise then, that in their interpretations of the universe, ancient thinkers reached for such ideals, regular and symmetrical objects and they preferred movements that proscribed perfect geometrical orbits or trajectories. In their opinion, these allowed them to better understand how the world works, or should work, but also to explain and predict the positions of individual objects. The ancient image of

harmony, this perfection which gives us pleasure. The sole thing to be feared in this respect is to use it too often" (Leibniz 1694-1698a, 83).

the universe is symmetrical and governed by the laws of symmetry. However, as multiple examples from the history of science show, enthralment by simple symmetry often led to limitations and the hiding of greater findings and symmetries.[28]

A distinctive example of the symmetry of planar objects are tiles. These, too, are related to ancient geometry and architecture, being, in fact, an invention thereof. Tiles cover a planar surface in such a way that they do not overlap and do not leave empty spaces. For this, it is important that they are of similar shapes or utilize an ingenious structure when they are laid. "In its sophisticated form, the mosaic has recognizable patterns, which are repeated in two different directions, where no centre, no boundary, no preferred direction, and no focus, is identified. The pattern of a mosaic work gives a sense of infinity" (Teicher 2012). And though Greek and Roman artists were aware of the art of the mosaic, it primarily brought fame to Arabian scholars responsible for the decorations of the Muslim Fort Alhambra in Granada.

"The Dutch artist M. C. Escher paid two visits to the Alhambra to sketch and catalogue the ornate patterns that can be found in the tiling throughout the palace and surrounding courtyards. Escher's tiling is not necessarily periodic, meaning that the tiles do not appear or occur at regular intervals. In the late 19th century it was proven that, from a mathematical point of view, there are only seventeen possible symmetries. In the early 20th century, it was discovered that the tiling in the Alhambra represents all of the seventeen possible symmetries! Hundreds of years of skilled construction, tiling, a deep respect for symmetry (as a harmonious force), and the study and knowledge of geometry (for religion as well as for commerce) resulted in all seventeen possible groups of symmetry being represented on the walls of the Alhambra! In 1944, the assertion that all seventeen symmetries could be found was challenged, but lately, once flexibilities of colours and interlacing were introduced, it was verified again" (Teicher 2012).

Escher, and the mathematician Roger Penrose later, created complicated periodic and non-periodic tiling of a plane using a finite set of basic tile types. Penrose tiling is invariant to the centre rotation, can show reflection and translational symmetry, is often non-periodic, self-similar (i.e. its patterns appear on multiple scales) and in theory each of its finite parts appear an infinite number of times in the whole. However, it does

28 Bacon criticized the prioritization of symmetries in this way in the negative part of the *Novum Organum Scientiarum*, and Kepler regretted his fascination for simple symmetries later in his life.

not use pentagons - the foundation of Pythagorean geometry. Since no tiling pattern using classical geometric shapes in an infinite arrangement could show fivefold symmetry, Penrose came up with his own shapes of tile to solve this issue. Their shapes, derived from the golden ratio, is not their only peculiarity - another is that the ratio of the tiles used correlates with the golden ratio. Additionally, as it was later discovered they can also be used to understand the existence of spatial quasicrystals with fivefold symmetry. This is the case as complicated periodic tiling resemble fractals.

Fractals are highly complex, yet carefully structured geometric shapes. Their characteristic feature is that their building blocks repeat non-periodically and form shapes that can be repeatedly observed on various levels and in various scales, even in such a way that the basic shapes can be infinitely embedded into themselves. This can be seen, for example, in the Koch snowflake, a geometric shape which we arrive at by iterations that start from an equilateral triangle, adding a tip of a triangle to the side on each iteration. The resulting shape then has a finite surface area, yet an infinite circumference. Examples of such fractals in nature are clouds, mountains, coastlines, snowflakes, but also the shells of nautili, plant leaves, tree branches, the structure of ferns, rivers, blood vessels, etc., that is, the most complicated and at first glance irregular objects. Despite their great diversity and complexity, it is becoming evident that what defines them mathematically is a relatively simple function - a certain rule that repeats recursively in their construction. Finding this rule is what is of relevance.

While in the regular aesthetics of geometric shapes, ornaments or natural structures we can often find the mentioned symmetries and laws of balance relatively easily and sometimes even spontaneously, in other (more complex) situations, the rule of orderliness, even order itself, may not be perceived or even discerned. On the contrary, it often must be revealed or explained to us for its perception to be possible. That is why, if we backtrack to the list of mathematical equations, which the scientists consider to be so beautiful, the crux of their attractiveness lies in the revelation of order and symmetry, again, in a rather symmetrical way.[29]

The essence of an equation, as such, is an expression of the dependences between something unknown and something else - something known. It is

29 The mathematical generalization of symmetry is group theory, formulated by the French mathematician Évariste Galois. "Galois first showed that every equation has its 'symmetric profile' - a group of permutations (today known as a Galois group), which stands for the symmetric attributes of the equation. The significance of this step is invaluable. Before Galois, equations were only sorted based on their degree: quadratic, cubic, quintic, etc. Galois discovered that the most important characteristic is symmetry" (Livio 2008, 168–169).

assumed that the right side of an equation is equal to the left, i.e. the contents are equivalent. The most basic equation, therefore, only states that the left and right sides are equal. For the sake of simplicity, this is usually expressed in such a way that the equality is seen (e.g. A=A). Such equations are therefore an example of both formal and content symmetry. The equality of both sides and the orderliness of the whole can be seen without any hint.

The situation becomes more complicated when one of the sides hides its symmetry and orderliness. We then hold a certain opinion, which grasps the given object or situation, but are not able to capture it through the perception of its order. We do not know what and how we grasp it; the symmetry and order elude us. A classic example of such a seemingly asymmetrical perception of things is the Pythagorean right-angle triangle. When we look at it, we see its geometric form, its shape, the right angle, but we do not know anything about its internal order (the sizes of its individual sides). At first sight, it may appear to be a random entity, the properties of which we do not know. However, when we acquaint ourselves with the Pythagoras's theorem, we will discover that there is a remarkable regularity between the lengths of the individual sides of a right-angle triangle, which can be expressed both arithmetically and geometrically. We can even ascertain for ourselves that the square of the length of the hypotenuse is equal to the sum of the squares of the lengths of the catheti by means of a geometrical or arithmetical proof, in which we will see that the square of the numerical value of the length of the hypotenuse is equal to the sum of the squares of the values of the lengths of the catheti ($a^2=b^2+c^2$). What we then see is a certain unusual symmetry which does not at first resemble symmetry (the right side of the equation does not look the same as the left). Only by understanding it can we see that this is a case of the content equality of both sides and therefore a type of symmetry, albeit one formally represented by different notations. The right side is the same as the left, but they do not look the same.

2.3. Knowledge – the Metaphor of Symmetry

The logician, mathematician and computer scientist Roger Antonsen (2016) believes that the essence of mathematics lies not only in the identification of patterns (units, links, structures, regularities and rules with uniform meanings, which govern what we see), but also in the creation of presumptions that something is one way or another, that it is governed by a set of rules, and last but not least - in the practical creation of remarkable things. He believes that the essence of understanding (even if only mathematical) is the ability to see things and phenomena from various perspectives and identify links. This is what mathematics does through equations. It finds links - metaphors between perceived or observed objects and new correlations from another perspective. This allows us to identify the 4:3 ratio not only in the cathetus of a right-angle triangle, where the hypotenuse five, in tone pitch and their mutual correlations, in rhythm, but also in the volume of a sphere in the multiplication of the third exponent of its radius, as well as in certain rules that apply to tetrahedrons and octahedrons. Platonic solids such as tetrahedrons, hexahedrons (a cube), octahedrons, dodecahedrons or icosahedrons may appear to be different from different perspectives. A tetrahedron is composed of triangles, as are octahedrons and icosahedrons. However, from any direct view, a tetrahedron resembles its triangle base, which is not the case for octahedrons or icosahedrons. From a certain perspective, an octahedron looks like a square, from other points of view like a rhombus and from yet further perspectives even more complex (pentagon, octagon), but always completely different. By changing our angle of view of the object, we also inevitably change the axes of the perceived symmetries, allowing new and perhaps unexpected views to appear. Without them, our understanding of an octagon would be very limited and erroneous.

One of the principles of visibility, whether we like it or not, is that from a single look at non-transparent objects we can never see more than three sides simultaneously. Thus, objects with multiple faces do not allow us to observe the whole of them, forcing us to observe them from several angles or at least to rotate them in our minds, to avoid hasty simplifications and distortions (e.g. that an octahedron is a triangle, tetragon, pentagon, octagon, or all at once). However, in order to understand a three-dimensional geometric object, inevitably we have to see it from several angles and to safely distinguish it from other objects. Only then can we speak of true understanding.

Roger Antonsen likens understanding to the ability to change perspectives and observe new symmetries (Antonsen 2016). Each new perspective or each discovery of a symmetry from a new perspective elevates the degree of understanding of an object and introduces it into a broader context. Naturally, it is possible to understand, for instance, the ocean with a look from the beach, where we can see the shape and periodicity of the waves and the correlation between them, where we can hear the sounds, smell it, feel the humidity, but we cannot see the immense size of the ocean or its structure as well as we could by looking down from an airplane. It seems apparent that in order to reach the full potential of possible comprehension, we must observe all of the possible perspectives and discover all of the regularities, rules and symmetries. But very often we do not have the time or opportunity to do that. Hence, scientists prefer the most representative perspectives, which undoubtedly include the view from within. In the case of oceans, it is the perspective from where we can feel the waves, their movement, humidity, power, pressure, smell, etc.; when diving, we may see its immense depth and optical or hydrostatic qualities. In mathematics such a perspective, from within, is the view of the mathematician (insiders),[30] who reflect upon the laws and principles of mathematics that they are familiar with, which they assess for the specific case and which are available to them. Quite understandably, the most valuable perspectives for scientists, of all the possible perspectives, are those which provide not only the most extensive insight into a problem, but also the one which consumes the least energy, or that in which the energy demanded leads to the greatest informational profit. In other words, what we desire the most is a perspective which, from a single look, contains as many diverse facts about an object and the links between them as possible.

Returning back to the beauties contained in mathematics, we will find that most elegant equations are written in such a way that the shortest expression is on one side (preferably with a single symbol) and the other contains its most simple representation by means of another, known expression. What we like about these notations is the level of their orderliness and degree of complexity. And it is obvious that the shorter an equation is, with a smaller number of symbols, the more elegant we consider it.

Recognizing beauty (not only in mathematics) can thus be compared to the revelation of symmetries and algorithms of orderliness. Sometimes, we find symmetry without realizing the individual operations that lead to it (such as finding the axis of symmetry); other times, we expect certain operations to be able to show us the hidden symmetry.

In the following chapters, we will therefore focus on such an understanding of beauty that is based on a mathematical approach for the understanding of beauty perception, its mathematical expression and possibly generation.

30 As opposed to the outsider.

3. Beauty as a Calculation

Although most art theoreticians do not consider beauty and aesthetic judgements to be an intentional and rational activity based on calculation, in the field of cognitive sciences there is growth in the popularity of the opinion that beauty perception, feeling, but also the production of aesthetic judgements or even works of art can be explained by the language of the logical-terminological inventory of mathematics and applied informatics. With a study by Roddie Cowie, *Beauty Is Felt, Not Calculated; and It Does Not Fit in Boxes* (Cowie 2014, 89–105) in mind, in this text we will try to show that beauty, its perception, experience and expectation, even such phenomena as taste and fashion, are processes which cannot only be explained by mathematical mental schemes, but which, in their essence, are based on a certain form of calculation, algorithms and computing (Beauty Is Felt, Because It Is Calculated).

Theories that interpret beauty and perception (especially the perception of visual stimuli) by mathematical means are in no way new or surprising. They can be encountered as early as the Pythagoreans,[31] Polykleitos' *Canon*,[32] Vitruvius,[33] but also in the Middle Ages[34] and were also popular in the Renaissance.[35] In recent years, especially under the influence of ap-

31 Theon of Smyrna and Archytas believed that beauty is an expression of the relation of proportionality, consonance and harmony and that it is expressible by numbers (Eco 2005, 62).

32 Polykleitos of Argos (480–410 BCE) was an influential ancient sculptor, who wrote what was possibly the first book on sculpture, titles *Canon* (Gr. κανών), in which he listed the norms for the portrayal of the human body. The book did not survive - however, multiple sculptures or their replicas did (e.g. Doryphoros). By measuring these, it was possible to reconstruct Polykleitos' ideal of proportions.

33 Vitruvius assumed that the composition of a beautiful work of architecture is founded on symmetry and the correct proportions (αναλογία) of the individual parts to the structure as a whole. As an example, he listed the correct proportions of the individual body parts: the head should form one-eighth of the entire height of the body, the face one-tenth, from the top of the chest to the top of the head is one-sixth of the height of a man, from the top of the chest to the hairline is one-seventh of the height of a man and the maximum width of the shoulders is a quarter of the height of a man. The distance from the breasts to the top of the head is a quarter of the height of a man, the distance from the elbow to the tip of the hand is a quarter of the height of a man, the distance from the elbow to the armpit is one-eighth of the height of a man, the length of the hand is one-tenth of the height of a man, the root of the penis is at half the height of a man, the foot is one-seventh of the height of a man and from the sole of the foot to below the knee is a quarter of the height of a man, from below the knee to the root of the penis is a quarter of the height of a man, the distances from below the chin to the nose and the eyebrows and the hairline are equal to the ears and to one-third of the face (Vitruvius 30 - 15 b. C.): *De architectura* 3.1.2–3.

34 Boethius in his *De arithmetika*, or the treatise on the construction of human and animal heads from the *Sketchbook* of Villard de Honnecourt (1235).

35 Leonardo da Vinci illustrated and modified the *Vitruvian Man* (probably after Giacomo Andrea de Ferrara and Francesco di Giorgio), showing the man in static and dynamic positions so that his outstretched extremities touch a circumscribed circle and the sides of

proaches using artificial intelligence and the cognitive sciences, there have appeared more and more scientific studies that understand beauty as a process of calculation (O'Toole 2011), but also that reveal the algorithms of perception and some of the variables relevant to this process (Cottrell Hsiao, 2011). Scientists and informaticists not only seek the laws of nature (they observe proportions, elements and contexts), study how perception takes place, but also suggest and test various systems to differentiate and evaluate visual stimuli, create artificial retinas, recognition programs and systems for modelling the most aesthetically suitable objects. And not only that - they try to not only reveal these mechanisms, but to apply the findings obtained in practice, even in such a way that they teach others to identify these algorithms, to master them and subsequently apply them in the production of works of art or other reproductions of specific artistic styles or methods. The recognition of the art created by a particular painter, his knacks, his way of seeing the world and elaboration of artworks is not only reserved for trained experts and art critics. It is becoming a part of a unique form of art - art which produces or transforms that, which was produced, according to the algorithms of a certain artistic method, and in such a way creates something new, yet based on well-tried methods.

3.1. Computational Aesthetics

According to Fuminori Akiba, computational aesthetics already has a long history (Scha and Bod 1993, Hoenig 2005). As early as 1928, G. D. Birkhoff introduced the concept of aesthetic measure (M) and defined it as a quantitative approach to various aesthetic fields - polygonal forms, ornaments and tiling, vases, harmony, melody and the musical quality of poetry. His fundamental thesis was that aesthetic measure depends upon the density of the elements of order in the aesthetic object, it is a ratio between order (O) and complexity (C): $M=O/C$ (Akiba 2013).[36] According to

a square. The centre of his body is his navel, and Leonardo obviously repeatedly utilized the golden ratio (the ratio of the distance of crown of the head and navel to the distance from the navel to the base). Another example of studying proportionality is Albrecht Dürer's *Four Books on Human Proportion* from 1528 or Luca Pacioli's work on the golden ratio (*De divina proportione - 1509*).

36 According to Birkhoff, aesthetic experience consists of three primary consecutive stages: "... (1) a preliminary effort of attention, which is necessary for the act of perception, and

Birkhoff, the more organized (ordered) the given object, the higher the aesthetic measure of the given degree of complexity. On the contrary, if there is a specified degree of order, then the aesthetic measure will be inversely proportional to the object's complexity. This means that, for instance, a square among quadrilaterals will show the highest degree of order which surpasses that of the rectangle or rhombus as it shows the highest degree of order at the same level of complexity.

Birkhoff explained his understanding of aesthetic measure with the example of simple polygons. He proposed that the aesthetic measure of polygons be calculated using the formula: $M=O/C=(V + E + R + HV-F)/C$, where C is the complexity of a polygon and polygonal order (O) is given by the vertical symmetry (V) of the object, polygonal equilibrium (E), rotational symmetry (R), horizontal and vertical (HV) grid and pleasing or unpleasing form (F). Polygonal complexity is defined by the quantity of lines on which all the edges of the polygon lie. Consequently, the more structured a polygon is, the higher its complexity. Vertical symmetry expresses symmetry about the vertical axis; rotational symmetry expresses the number of axes which symmetrically divide the polygon. The more symmetrical an object is (the higher the number of axes of symmetry), the higher its degree of order. The value of HV (horizontal and vertical grid) is related to the potential movement of polygons over a plane. HV is considered to be positive if the polygon can move vertically or horizontally into a new position while preserving its relative position within an identical horizontal and vertical grid. The higher the number of possibilities for the incorporation of an element into its environment, the higher the HV value.[37] The equilibrium (E) of a given polygon expresses the feeling of the visual equilibrium of the shape (neither geometric, nor physical); the form of the overall impression (F) is represented by values from 1 through 0 to -1, according to whether the polygon evokes pleasant or unpleasant emotions. The ultimate aesthetic measure is thus a matter of our capability to identify the level of complexity, as well as the order, in a given object, which are represented by various types of symmetry, its integration into a visual context and the overall object equilibrium. Therefore, the most symmetrical objects have the highest value of aesthetic measure dependent on the level of complexity of the given object.

---

which increases in proportion to what we shall call the complexity C of the object; (2) the feeling of value or aesthetic measure (M) which rewards this effort; and finally (3) a realization that the object is characterized by a certain harmony, symmetry, or order (O), more or less concealed, which seems necessary to aesthetic effect" (Birkhoff 1933, 3–4).

37 For more specific attribution of values of specific polygon aspects, cf. Douchová 2016.

Birkhoff was aware that the overall aesthetic measure is dependent on multiple factors (size, colour, structure, etc.) and, therefore, he merely focused on its identification in relatively simple polygons. He presented his contribution at the International Congress of Mathematicians in Bologna, 1928, and published it in *The World of Mathematics,* edited by J. Newman (1933). Even though he caught the attention of numerous psychologists, Birkhoff's concept was soon forgotten, probably due to the lack of complexity of all the assessed factors of a stimulus, as well as the lack of experimental verification, that is, negative results from aesthetic experiments based on his predictions. In 1968, Harold J. McWhinnie picked up this theory in his own work *A Review of Research on Aesthetic Measure*, which, however, inclined more towards the prediction of aesthetic preferences than to an investigation of the aesthetic measure of individual objects.

As Veronika Douchová points out, Abraham Moles came up with a modification of Birkhoff's concept in 1958. "Inspired by Shannon's mathematical theory of communication, he developed Birkhoff's ideas into a theory of information and aesthetic perception. He redefined Birkhoff's aesthetic measure from the ratio of order O and complexity C to their multiplication O×C. The original notion of order O in Birkhoff's measure takes in Moles' work, the form of low entropy, perceived as redundancy and predictability. High entropy is equated with complexity C, perceived as unpredictability and non-compressibility" (Douchová 2016, 48).

Max Bense and Frieder Nake had similar ideas and observed the relationships between aesthetics and information processing and information theory. Bense suggested the utilization of both Shanahan's entropy and the redundancy principle, since he was convinced that creative processes, as well as the perception of aesthetic objects, are based on a limited repertoire of elements and therefore on a selective process. The percipient neglects multiple unimportant aspects and elements, while the creator selects from a certain set of realizable elements and processes. "For instance, if the repertoire is given by a palette of colours with a probability distribution, the final product (in our case, a painting) is a selection (a realization) of this palette on a canvas. Although the distribution of elements of an aesthetic state has a certain order, the repertoire shows a certain complexity" (Rigau et al. 2008, 27). Bense thus distinguished between global and partial complexity, and, similarly, between global and partial order.

Considering the fact that Birkhoff's original equation of aesthetic measure assumed the complexity of an aesthetic object as a denominator, it is only natural that theoreticians assumed an inverse proportionality between aesthetic value and the complexity of organization and expression of the assessed phenomenon. In the 1990s, Jürgen Schmidhuber described an algorithmic theory of beauty which takes the subjectivity of the observer into account and postulates: among several observations classified as comparable by a given subjective observer, the aesthetically most pleasing is the one with the shortest description, given the observer's previous knowledge and his particular method of encoding the data (Schmidhuber 1997). In other words, the most aesthetically valuable objects are those that can be distinguished and subsequently described by a relatively small amount of information (bits). Schmidhuber's theory distinguishes between what is beautiful and what is interesting; it also claims that interestingness corresponds with the derivation of subjectively perceived beauty. This theory is based on an assumption that a percipient who attempts to comprehend and grasp the object he is viewing prefers epistemologically and energetically less demanding solutions to this problem through finding or formulating regularities and rules, according to which the given objects can be organized or by means of which it is possible to explain the given object. Such rules include successions, repetitions, symmetries, similarities and any other aspects that can be formulated as rules. It is only natural that we prefer to use the simplest rules for the explanation of complex phenomena. Therefore, when we see for instance a face, we try to focus on those regularities that are most characteristic of it and that would, at the same time, distinguish it from other similar objects. If we can find an algorithm that leads to an improvement in the compression[38] of data necessary for assessments in a way that the observation can be carried out in a more economical way than previously, we experience an intellectual reward in the form of curiosity saturation (Schmidhuber 1991).

In his book, *The Paradox of Choice,* psychologist Barry Schwartz described a remarkable phenomenon, of the scarcity and redundancy of information and the possibility of successful selection. He found that a client confronted with an offer of 175 types of salad dressing was incapable of choice, the choice being highly demanding and ultimately unsuccessful (he was not satisfied and does not know if he ordered the right one). This is related to the fact that if we must order and assess too many options and elements, we use too much energy and ultimately the ability to choose is paralyzed. Twenty years after his book was published, Californian scientists Colin Camerer, Caltech, and Robert Kirby, Professor of Behavioral Economics and the T&C Chen Center for Social and Decision Neuroscience

38 He understands compressibility in terms of Kolmogorov complexity theory – the briefest description of data, from which it is possible to retrieve the original data.

Leadership, confirmed that "Choice overload reduces neural signatures of choice set value in the dorsal striatum and anterior cingulate cortex", or, in other words, that too many choices complicate the ability to calculate the potential rewards and discourage decision-making. "The fMRI scans revealed brain activity in two regions while the participants were making their choices: the anterior cingulate cortex (ACC), where the potential costs and benefits of decisions are weighed; and the striatum, a part of the brain responsible for determining value. Camerer and his colleagues also saw that activity in these two regions was highest in subjects who had 12 options to pick from, and lowest in those with either six or 24 items to choose from. The pattern of activity is probably the result of the striatum and the ACC interacting and weighing the increasing potential for reward (getting a picture they really like for their mug) against the increasing amount of work the brain will have to do to evaluate possible outcomes" (Reutskaja, Lindtner, Nagel 2018). This led scientists to the conclusion that an optimal number of options is in an interval ranging from 8 to 15 elements, correlating with well-known facts related to memory capacity that can retain 7+/- 2 elements. We perceive a lower number of elements as limited and too simple, yet higher number of elements force a continuous verification of previous options, since we cannot retain and compare them. Therefore, it is possible to consider analogous reasons why people do not usually prefer extremely complex and complicated aesthetic objects, but they opt for those of a lower or at most a moderate degree of complexity, since it does not demand so much energy to grasp and retain it, that is, the benefit from the perception of such beauty is not devalued by an exceedingly high demand on both the intellect and our energy to allow its identification and perception.

An example of such energy calculation is minimalism. It includes the highest ratio of order and complexity. This might be why, besides others, very intelligent people consider the formal records of frequently complex phenomena which are as simple as possible in terms of their form to be beautiful (and, inadvertently truthful). This is true for art, as well as science. "Mathematicians talk of "beautiful", "deep", "insightful", and "interesting" proofs, and award each other prizes on the basis of these assessments" (Inglis, Aberdein 2014). By the term "beauty", they frequently mean simplicity, brevity and elegance. "The most important determinant of a proof's perceived beauty is thus the degree to which it lends itself to being grasped in a single act of mental apprehension" (McAlister 2005, 22). "Similarly, Michael Atiyah claims that "elegance is more or less synonymous with simplicity" (cited in (Wells 1990, 39), and similar views can be found in the works of Carl Friedrich Gauss (e.g. Tappenden 2008), Werner

Heisenberg (e.g. Engler 1990) and Poincare (e.g. Chandrasekhar 2010), as well as many other contemporary research mathematicians (e.g. Cherniwchan et al. 2013)" - cited in (Inglis, Aberdein 2014, 89). It is obvious that precision, validity, reliability of formulation or proof represent no less important values of scientific knowledge, yet in the case of the comparability of the aforementioned attributes of two formulations, we arbitrary tend to opt for that formulation, which is aesthetically more elegant, i.e. energetically less demanding. That is why memes have multiplied throughout the history of art and culture primarily by simplification and energy-efficient replication. Simplicity is an attribute that is attractive, and numerous theoreticians believe that beauty indeed lies in simplicity (Glynn 2010).[39]

Works by Moles, Bense and others finally led to the establishment of Information Aesthetics and a scientific effort to create a mathematically rigid aesthetic theory without subjective elements (Nake 2012). This approach was founded on information theory, semiotics and communication theory. The most famous protagonist of this movement was probably Frieder Nake, who, together with A. Michael Noll and Georg Nees, designed software for the production of artistic drawings. The first public exhibitions of artworks produced using this software took place from 5th to 19th February 1965, at the Technische Hochschule in Stuttgart, Germany; 6th to 24th April 1965, at the Howard Wise Gallery in New York and from 5th to 26th November 1965. They became a common, integral part of some exhibitions from 1969 onwards (including the 35th Venice Biennale (Italy, 1970) and Arteonica (São Paulo, Brazil, 1971)).

"Now multiple societies for computational aesthetics exist such as Computational Aesthetics in Graphics, Visualization and Imaging (CAe) and the International Society for Mathematical and Computational Aesthetics (IS-MCA). The latter in particular covers a wide scope: computer-aided design and manufacturing, design of robotic motion, the analysis of artistic masterpieces, scientific theory building and reasoning, and software design" (Akiba 2013, 119).

Since the beginning of the millennium, there has been an increase in the interest in the algorithmization of beauty, the mathematical analysis of symmetry, purpose, complexity or simplicity, repetition, etc., and even attempts to define computational aesthetics (e.g. Hoenig 2005; or the mechanisms of computational aesthetic assessment - Galanter 2012) and to

39 However, as other scientists (Inglis, Aberdein 2014, 102-103) have demonstrated, simplicity does not guarantee beauty (it is rather an obstacle to precision), and mathematicians use the term "simplicity" a bit differently to philosophers.

create software which would be able to deduce and predict the aesthetic quality of objects (Datta et al. 2006; Wong et al. 2009; Wu et al. 2010; Faria et al. 2013). The majority utilize the principles of machine learning and image comparison with those objects that have already been identified as aesthetically valuable by the users. This approach resulted, for instance, in the creation of the software, *The Acquine Engine* (2009), that assesses photographs taken by the users, or the latest research project ALIPR led by James Z. Wang at Pennsylvania State University. This project is oriented towards the creation of a sufficiently large database of visual data to allow the exploration of algorithms for ideal form and visual composition, emotionality and works of art, e.g. by Vincent van Gogh. The utilization of IT is undergoing very dynamic development, further supported by neuromarketing and applied aesthetics due to its potential for exact and easily quantifiable research.

Probably the most important proponent of a computational approach to art is Alex J. Champandard, who created the software programme *Deep Forger*[40] that modifies optical visual originals (e.g. photos) into a form where they appear to have been produced by an artist in one of various artistic styles. In such a way, it is possible to create new Van Goghs, Picassos or Klimts and thus eternalize one's sceneries or objects in the styles of various artists.[41] Even more, it is possible to not only modify the "artistic object" in a certain style, but also to create it from scratch. Ahmed Elgammal and his team at the Art and Artificial Intelligence Laboratory at Rutgers University observed more than 62,000 paintings and analysed the aspects they have in common, as well as those in which they differ (2015). By observing common characteristics, identical features, methods, contents and means, we can identify the author's style and character, his individual viewpoint

40 *Deep Forger* can be found on Twitter (https://twitter.com/deepforger); and Google created its own version of this software called *Deep Dream*, indicating that art from artificial intelligence is slowly becoming a specific branch of business and the art industry.

41 *Deep Forger* works on basis of Deep Neutral Nets - deep neural networks and deep learning. Based on the immense database of digitalized non-artistic, as well as artistic images of all historical periods (Big Data), it gradually learns to recognize, categorize, compare and generate (not create, but digitally form in a generative way) pictures using neural algorithms. It, for instance, re-programs a photo into a "graphics" or a "painting". Or, it re-programs the image without (identified author's) - or from one identified style - into another one. It thus allows for more than a 75 % success in software recognition and therefore also in the classification of artistic works (e.g. Picasso - Matisse). Yet, all the operations with the tremendous amount of images are done in the binary code, in contrast to humans, which work with a much lower number of images using their senses, mainly the sight. Even a computer which would have input from its camera (visual recording) would be able to translate it to the binary code and back.

and the manner in which he expresses his ideas. Consequently, it is also possible to imitate him. Vice versa, by observing the differences between exquisite artworks, Elgammal and his colleagues identified an algorithm for the determination and measurement of the creativity and degree of novelty of any given artwork.[42] According to him, it is not only possible to evaluate the novelty and originality of the methods, but also to programme a generation of new artworks utilizing this knowledge.[43]

This is not only true for visual art. In a similar way to paintings, one can compose new pieces of music reflecting the style, instrumentation, pace, mood and duration (e.g. *Ampermusic* – Pogue 2018); and an expansion of such technologies to other forms of art can also be expected.

The foundations of the computational approach to music production do not only lie in musical structures that can be described mathematically (from the Pythagorean understanding of tones as the length ratio of vibrating strings – through precise mathematical expressions of height (frequencies), length (duration), force (amplitude), colour (the spectral compo-

42 Elgammal's and Sahel's program tries to appraise creativity by computer based on the comparison between so-called subjective creativity – the originality of the artwork based on the context of its creation, and so-called objective – historical creativity, which expresses the impact of artwork on other artworks by different artists. Therefore, it does not only appraise creativity based on a certain specific artistic or psychologic definition of creativity or style, but it also compares the used styles and determines the computational creativity of different artworks. Originality is measured there in comparison to the previous artworks, which share no elements with the examined one, and the impact of the artwork is expressed in comparison to the artworks created after the creation of the examined artwork and share its elements and "signature". Elgammal's and Sahel's algorithm, therefore, does not compare the artworks within the framework of individual art-historical and art-scientific frames and conceptions, but it compares them without supervision – by comparison of different parameters and their importance considering the limited amount of patterns. The essence of their algorithm is in moving the artwork into the future – this creativity is impactful. Their algorithm moves the images from the year of their creation into the past and the future (like the time machine) and if it finds comparable images in a certain time period, it appraises the moved ones as creative: the most creative image of its age was Munch's *The Scream* and Malevich's *Red Square*.

43 There are some problems with the algorithm they use, for example, 1) it only manipulates with publically accessible digitalized images – data (closed world limit – the limit of the closed world of the contemporarily accessible images: it does not have any data from private galleries nor from galleries with a special regime of unpublished artworks); 2) it has its limits when it comes to artistic concepts of vision and the image: it only works with the image which is optically captured by a machine (it has no data about human vision, sight and its concepts, its importance in art, etc.); 3) it is limited by parametrization: the parameter settings: space, texture, shape, colour... every new adaptation of the amount and importance of the "concepts" and "parameters" can lead to a different result in appraising creativity as well as to a different interpretation of different criteria. The results of this new appraising will thus be changed in the future as a result of this change in the limits and parameters.

sition of the sound of individual tones) and their ratios and harmony and rhythms), but also mainly in the logic of composition and musical thinking. If we listen to a piece of music, frequently, we are capable not only of the identification of the author on the basis of previous experience, but also the assumption of potential directions, rhythms and musical escalations in new pieces. This takes place because we anticipate a certain musical logic that we observed from what we had just listened to and from previous musical experiences. Simultaneously, we are aware of a certain diapason of potential elements and continuations. In other words: we combine elements and we utilize elements of Bayesian probability in our combinatorics. In such a way, it is also possible to teach machines to "observe and copy" the logic of individual authors, the musical instruments they utilize most often, their rhythms, phrases and thus to produce new variations, themes or compositions of a given author. Furthermore, in the case of machine learning and computational music, it is possible to test matters that a human subject would probably not be able to (unlikely musical solutions) and thus to explore entirely new kinds of music.

3.2. Perception as a Calculation

The following chapter will focus on defending the fundamental thesis that aesthetic perception is a calculation not only in the sense that the perception of art and the intentional search for individual stimuli (a visit to a gallery) is related to certain calculations of the amount of potential pleasure - reward system calculations - but also in a sense that it is possible to reflect on perception using the language of algorithms and calculations on the level of the retina, cortex, as well as on the level of the motivation to search for it.

Our first-level reflection is an outline of how perception originates at all, starting at its most basic level - the retina.

Primary theories of perception include several models of perception comprehension, among which the key players are bottom-up theories, top-down constructivist concepts, synthesizing models as well as computational perception theories (Rookes, Willson 2007, Démuth 2013a). Computational theories (e.g. Marr's theory of perception) are based on the belief that the perception process can be successfully explained by means of calculating operations and computation itself is not a metaphor by which the phenomenon can be explained, but our sensory apparatus actually works in a computation way. One great example of such an explanation is the clarification of colour stimulus origin in bipolar cells in deeper retinal structures.

As we know, a healthy human retina contains two essential types of photosensitive cells - rods and cones that differ not only in their morphological structure and functionality, but also in location. Rods are sensitive to the amount of incident light, yet these cells do not respond to its wavelength (white-and-black vision). "While rhodopsin included in the rods allows for the perception of light in a light-dark scale (chiaroscuro), iodopsin derivatives included in the cones (approx. 6–7 million) allow a response to the incident light according to its wavelength and thus allow the perception of colours" (Démuth 2013a, 35). In simplified words: brightness of the final picture corresponds with the level of excitation of specific rods, and the final chroma of the perceived object corresponds with the level and ratio of excitation of individual cones. The fundamental fact of colour perception is that all cones respond to all incident light; however, they do so according to which of the three types of iodopsin they contain, which are sensitive to various wavelengths, reaching their maximum levels in either the fields of blue, red or green light. Therefore, at this level, colour mixing occurs and a "calculation" of the overall colour according to the structure and illumination intensity. "Since each cone can react to the entire spectrum of visible light but with varying intensity in specific areas, no cone is directly responsible for the ultimate colour. That is obtained by a comparison of the excitation of individual cones. Additive and subtractive cells serve this purpose in the retina. Additive signals from the cones join and subtractive cells respond only when the nerve potentials in both neighbouring cones are not identical. Medium and long wavelength cones create a circuit consisting of a pair of subtraction cells and an additive cell. If a cone sensitive to medium wavelengths is more highly activated within the pair of two mutually joined cones, a subtractive cell is activated, which sends the signal related to green colour perception to the brain. The second subtractive cell remains silent. This cell would only be activated if the cone sensitive to long wavelengths was more highly stimulated. The third type of cone - sensitive to short wavelengths - forms an individual circuit with another pair of subtractive cells and one additive cell. Remarkably both subtractive cells receive the signal from that cone and additive cell of the combined output of the previous circuit type (red-green). If the overall potential at the subtractive cells of the cone sensitive to short wavelengths is higher than in the additive cell, the brain receives a signal related to blue light incident on retina. If the potential at additive cell of this circuit is higher, the brain interprets the signal as yellow (Pollack 2003). However, if there is a non-zero potential in both subtractive cells of this circuit, both cells are silent. The additive cell in this circuit is activated and evaluates the activation of all three types of retinal cones as incident white light. Both basic Hering channels also saturate the function of white-black channel in such manner" (Démuth 2013a, 61–62). In other words: bipolar retinal cells perform a simple comparison of the excitation of individual cones and by binary comparison and interpretation, create the final colour. This explains why certain shades of colour can never be seen (reddish-green, bluish-yellow – either the red or the green channel is excited, but these two can never be excited simultaneously) even though the rest of the shade combinations does not represent a problem of perception for us. Therefore, colour is the result of simple mixing, respectively excitation and inhibition of individual processes and their mutual comparison.

This consideration method allows for the explanation of even very complex and multilevel mental states which are, at first glance, seemingly irreducible to basic binary processes by means of their division and analysis at individual levels in the form of a simple binary assessment (yes/no) and calculation. Finally, all states of the receptive cells can be transformed to the form of either "excited" or "non-excited", and the overall diversity of our mental world is just a variety of the combinations of these states.

The perception of a picture and its individual elements is not realized exclusively in the retina in any case. Essential processes occur in the visual cortex or the brain itself. Therefore, Edwin Land proposed a theory that localizes the perception of visual stimuli (colours in particular) between the retina and cortex; this is reflected in the title of his concept – the Retinex theory. Land was convinced that the processing of colour stimuli takes place through the comparison of three separate visual channels. He believed that colourful originals are perceived by means of visual cortex that separately assesses each surface according to how they are sensed individually by cones that are especially sensitive to the red spectrum, by cones especially sensitive to the blue spectrum and also separately by photosensitive cells that are especially sensitive to the green spectrum. Thus, it is as if we obtain three pictures of the visual fields, which we subsequently compare in the cortex. The peculiarity of this relative reflectance of the individual area calculation process, for which Land designed an algorithmic expression in the form of a formula,[44] is that the final colour of the perceived surface does not only depend on the activity of individual recep-

44 $R^{\lambda}_{(i;j)} = \sum_k \partial \log I_{(k+1)}/k$ (cf. Land 1983, 5167).

tors and their mutual comparisons, but also on extent of the reflectance of all the perceived surfaces within the entire visual field. This would mean that we not only compose the resulting colour of a given object according to the activity of the "red", "blue" or "green" channels, in the same way as polaroid camera via individual filters, but also that the colour of each specific stimulus is, to a certain extent, always dependent on the colour of all the other surfaces in the field of view. Land utilized this effect (bearing his name up to this day) to test the perception of colourful originals in a test based on Mondrian pictures. Clear colourful abstract originals eliminate the effects of the memory of colours, as labelled by Helmholz, as well as any potential associations with how we remember what colour certain objects have. Intellectual contamination of colour perception is a frequent question in disputes between conceptualists and non-conceptualists, associated with the issue of perception definition (Mcpherson 2012). It has been shown that the actual reflectances of individual surfaces are independent from the nature of the original, yet they demonstrate a certain dependence not only on the functionality of the aforementioned retinex channels, but also on the overall structure and reflectance of all the surfaces in the field of vision. This phenomenon was successfully tested by Oliver Sacks in the diagnosis of his patient who was a colour-blind painter (Sacks, Wasserman 1987).

Land's idea that the visual perception of individual stimuli originates in a data calculation somewhere between the retina and the cortex can similarly be applied to other object attributes, not merely their colour. Koch and Crick documented that hypothalamic scanning of excitation states of individual cortex neurons, which takes place four times per second, maps not only the actual state of the given neurons, but also the nature of their mutual relationships. Together, they came to the conclusion that the brain does not have to constantly calculate all the individual states, this would be highly inefficient; it is sufficient to do it only where it focuses. This means that the things we perceive do not include the whole vision field, but we perceive, in particular, those things which have changed since the last scan. The rest remain unchanged and thus somewhat unimportant. In such a manner, evolutionary epistemologists can explain why we are so sensitive to, for instance, the perception of changes in motion in our vision field, especially when they are directed towards us. It is obvious that perception of changes gives an advantage to an individual, warns him about possible upcoming dangers (e.g. the occurrence of predators) and thus it is prioritized in our consciousness. Numerous authors have become aware of this in art and have attempted to incorporate it, even in relatively static expositions.[45] Motion or the illusion of motion attracts attention; however, they do so only to the extent to which they can still surprise. We also become aware of this in our sense of touch. If we touch something new, we are attentive; if these touches are unchanging, monotonous and rhythmical and are of constant intensity, etc., we cease to be aware of them.

3.3. Beauty as a Calculation with an Unclear Solution Algorithm

Efforts to grasp and describe the attributes of beautiful objects have occurred in parallel with the interest of humankind in such objects. They have been strengthened by approaches pointing to the fact that although there may be a certain degree of variability in preferences for beautiful objects,[46] there is also significant agreement on our evaluation of the outside world from the viewpoint of beauty. Examples of this agreement include cross-cultural research on the ideal beautiful landscape (Hägerhäll et al. 2018), millions of different visitors that admire the same paintings in the Louvre or the figure of a model or an actress which is considered to be beautiful across several continents. A pregnant expression related to such an approach is the thesis that visual stimuli could have an intrinsic "significant form", which can elicit the perception of beauty (Bell 1914). Searching for evolutionarily or otherwise acquired objects or algorithms of aesthetic judgement has become a prominent domain of cognitive scientists and evolutionary epistemologists. Glenn Wilson (Wilson, Brazendale 1974), Devendra Singh (1993a, 1993b) and others have investigated the relationship between the circumferences of the chest, waist and hips and the perception of the attractiveness of a female figure. They observed that men of almost every age and culture consider those female figures with a waist-to-hip ratio of which is approx. 0.7:1 to be attractive (Singh, Young 2001, Freedman, Carter, Sbrocco et al. 2004, 2007). The reason for this lies in the age, fertility and state of health of the person with such a figure (usually, only women between the ages of 15 and 35 have such figures), whose physical appearance signalizes that

45 Certain artworks by Escher and Duchamp that evoke the impression of motion through hints that encourage the eyes to follow specific lines are examples of such a method.
46 This variability was emphasized by the representatives of subjectivist approaches, as characterized by the following quotations: "Beauty is in the eye of the beholder" (Hungerford 1878), or in Latin "de gustibus non disputandum est".

she has the appropriate hormone levels that correlate with fertility, their vitality and the probability that she will live to the age necessary for raising a child, and also other evolutionarily significant indicators of the suitability of the bearer of such figure for the investment of energy in her to maintain one's own genes (Fischer, Voracek 2006; Cornelissen 2009; Lutoslawska, Malara et. al. 2014; Wang Djafarian, Chima et. al. 2015). Therefore, evolutionary psychologists also observe numerous other features of attractiveness (the colour and structure of the complexion, hair length, the shape of the eyes, lips, eyebrows, eyelashes, etc.) believing that they will reveal and verbalize the hidden mechanisms of attractiveness that we have acquired throughout the evolution of both men and women, or directly in their environment, focusing on various elements or manifestations of attractiveness.

3.3.1. Calculations of the Beauty of Human Faces

The human face is an example that has long attracted the interest of researchers seeking to find the specific parameters of objects that evoke the experience of beauty. A considerable number of scientific studies, especially those conducted over the last decades, have brought recurring findings. Specifically, there has been an effort to measure beautiful faces, and thus express the mutual relationships between the individual features of a beautiful face (to quantify them) to enable the language of numbers and mathematics to express the characteristics of a beautiful face.

3.3.1.1. The History of the Examination of Facial Parameters

Although the history of the examination of the beauty of the human face has not left many calculations, or exact data that objectivizes this quality, it is obvious that the evaluation of facial beauty and the expression of what makes it beautiful has a rich history. On the basis of precise observations, many artists and painters have created a number of canons or guidelines on how to capture (paint, model) a human figure or face so that it looks beautiful (Naini, Moss, Gill 2006). These include the Egyptian canon, in which six times the length of the sole represented the optimum height for a human figure[47]

47 This canon was later modified to seven times; probably under the influence of ancient patterns (Petkovsky 2016).

(Petkovsky 2016), or the Vitruvian figure,[48] which later reappeared in a number of variations, e.g. in the Renaissance works of Albrecht Dürer and Leonardo da Vinci, as well as later, in the 19th century.

Efforts to grasp the mathematic proportions of the lengths of individual parts of the human body were accompanied by a mathematical focus on the face. The history of such efforts also dates back to ancient times, e.g. it is obvious from later records that Vitruvius also studied the proportions of the human head, typically applying a division into thirds. On the basis of his measurements, Leonardo da Vinci created a sketch of the proportions of the head, where this rule was applied several times. The face is divided into thirds - one third is the distance between the hairline and the eyebrows, the second third from the eyebrows to the base of the nose and the third from the base of the nose to the bottom of the chin. From the last third (the lower part of the face), a third is also represented by the upper lip. Similarly, the ear represents a third of the height of the face. In addition, the distance from the hairline to the upper part of the chin should represent a tenth of one's height (Naini, Moss, Gill 2006). Numerous guidelines on the portrayal of a beautiful human face have been formulated; common neoclassical canons relating to the proportions of the human face are presented in Tab. 1.

Franz Joseph Gall (1758–1828) and Johann Gaspar Spurzheim (1776–1832) are associated with later attempts at the more precise measurement of the human face. These phrenologists considered the size and shape of specific areas of the head including facial parts to be the key to the determination of the different characteristics of individuals. The popularity of this theory[49] in the 18th and the 19th centuries generated interest in the measurement of the distances and angles of individual parts of the head and human face, and it was also reflected in the first sophisticated devices and equipment designed for such measurements. These included an anthropometric device by Major A. J. N. Tremearne (1914), or Max Factor's "beauty calibrator" said to be able to measure facial beauty to a hundredth of an inch (Easton 2004).

---

48 Vitruvius was a Roman architect, who, in his treatise, *De Architectura,* outlined the ideal proportions of the human body (Tonelli 2013). It is a painting of a man with outspread arms, whose figure is inscribed inside both a circle and a square. These geometric shapes also serve as the reference framework for expressing the proportions of the lengths of individual parts of the body.

49 Which later became outdated and was rejected.

Tab. 1. Examples of neoclassical canons regarding the proportions of human faces (Kusugal 2015, 333)

Name of the canon	Equation	Description
Facial profile canon	tr-n=n-sn=sn-gn	The face can be divided into equal thirds, with the nose occupying the middle third.
Orbital canon	en-en=ex-en	The distance between the eyes is equal to the width of each eye.
Orbitonasal canon	en-en=al-al	The distance between the eyes is equal to the width of the nose.
Nasooral canon	ch-ch=1.5 (al-al)	The width of the mouth is one and one-half times the width of the nose.
Nasofacial canon	al-al=1/4 (zy-zy)	The width of the nose is one-fourth the width of the face.
Nasoaural canon	n-sn=sa-sba	The length of the nose is equal to the length of the ear.

Abbreviations used: tr-trichion, n-nasion, en-endocanthion, ex-exocanthion, zy-zygion, sn-subnasale, al-alare, ch-cheilion, gn-gnathion

3.3.1.2. Applying the Golden Ratio

The Ancient Greeks believed that beauty was represented by a golden ratio (Atalay, 2006). The golden ratio is an imaginary linear division where the proportion of the shorter part to the longer part (after division) is equal to the proportion of the longer part to the whole line (Green 1995). This relationship can be mathematically expressed by the formula: $a \div b = b \div (a + b)$, while $a + b = 1$. The presence of the "golden ratio" in objects (pentagrams, spirals, rectangles, etc.) ensured their visual beauty and perfection. Efforts to apply the golden ratio to other objects and to discover perfect, "divine proportions" thus was expanded to many other areas of life and human investigation; they affected philosophy, sculpture, architecture and painting, as well as music. The finding that the "golden ratio" could be found in the optimum proportions of the human figure was of crucial importance in the analysis of beauty. The work of the Greek sculptor Polykleitos (477–410) is an illustrative example. Although the theoretical basis for his creation of exquisitely elaborated sculptures has not been preserved, its practical form - embodied in the bronze statue of a young boy with a spear - is preserved in the form of copies of the statue (Petkovsky 2016).

The bronze statue of the figure of Dyofor is proportionally divided at the waist in the golden ratio (i.e. the ratio of the length of the body from the waist upwards to the length of the body from the waist downwards is equal to the ratio of the length of the body from the waist downwards to the total length of the body). In the same manner, the proportions of the lower limbs respect the golden ratio - the ratio of the length of the legs from the knee upwards (to the waist) to the length from the knee downwards equals to the ratio of the whole leg to the length of the knee upwards (to the waist). The canons of proportions were used with some variations in the works of Albrecht Dürer and Leonardo da Vinci, as well as later, in the 19th century. The German psychologist Adolf Zeising described the golden ratio as the aesthetic law of proportions (Herz-Fischler 2004), and created detailed calculations of the golden ratio as applied to the human body. For example, he stated that the distance from the crown to the navel is in the same ratio as the distance from the navel to the mat compared to the body height.

The golden ratio was thus used as an "ideal measure" in several areas, and was also applied in the examination of the beauty of the human face. In her book *The Geometry of Art and Life*, Matilda Ghyka (1946) described the occurrence of divine proportion in natural forms (shells, flowers), in geometric objects (pentagram, pentagon, star-decagon), as well as in human works (Byzantine cupolas, Great pyramid, etc.) and in particular, the human body. Particular attention was paid to the faces of Isabella d'Este[50] and the contemporary tennis player Helen Wills. These analyses were later used in the 1960s to create the first manuals used in the reconstruction of a severely deformed face (Shell, Woods 2004). As the divine proportions have been used in the area of facial reconstruction, they have also been promoted as a useful tool for the aesthetic restorative rehabilitation of dentition (see, e.g. Levin 1978).

Along with efforts to apply the golden ratio rule to facial beauty assessment or reconstruction surgery, critical studies that have invalidated the universal application of the golden ratio in aesthetics have occurred. Supporters of the existence of ideal proportions that correspond to the golden ratio have rejected them, claiming that several methodological issues were not adequately addressed in these studies. For example, opponents of the studies have used average proportions in their computations, although it is well-known that highly attractive facial configurations are not average. Furthermore, the complexity of facial configurations (e.g. in repose, smil-

50 The portrait of Isabella d'Este (known as "Isabella in Black") was painted by the Italian painter Titian (Tiziano Vecelli/Tiziano Vecellio) between 1534 and 1536.

ing and other expressions) were ignored. Finally, the proportions that tended to conform to the golden ratio in beautiful faces in previous research were (Tr-M):(Tr-Sn), (Tr-M):(N-M)[51] in repose and eye width: mouth width when smiling (Prokopakis et al. 2013).

In more recent research, Pallett, Link and Lee (2010) sought, through a series of experiments, to uncover the existence of an ideal composition of individual facial parts. In their experiments, they dealt with the distance between the eyes and mouth, thus changing the ratio of this distance to overall facial length[52] (i.e. changing the so-called length ratio). The second change was to the distance between pupils, which changed the ratio between this distance and facial width[53] (the so-called width ratio). In these experiments, where the participants evaluated the beauty of faces with different values of the aforementioned parameters, they sought to uncover an optimum ratio of facial length and width. They found that the facial distances assessed as beautiful did not correspond to the original value of the golden ratio (i.e. 1:1.618 - Atalay 2006). According to their results, the optimum vertical distance between the eyes and mouth represented approximately 36 % of the overall facial length, while the optimum horizontal distance between the eyes was approximately 40 % of the facial width (Pallett, Link, Lee 2010). Thus, they postulated "new" golden ratios, which differed from the Classical ratios.

Their efforts to apply the golden ratio to the examination of beauty were gradually abandoned and in addition to the verification of the validity of this "magic" ratio, researchers have also sought to identify new values for the ratios and distances for beautiful faces. In their latest research, Mantelakis et al. (2018) included six horizontal and seven vertical (Tab. 2) distances between individual facial parts in their measurements. The authors measured the given distances, uncovering the values of the mutual ratios between such measurements (they created twelve different ratios).

51 The abbreviations of the sizes of individual facial parts correspond to the terminology used in Table 1: "m" = menton.

52 The overall "facial length" (so-called length ratio) is measured as the distance between the hairline and the chin.

53 The overall "facial width" (so-called width ratio) is measured as the distance between the inner edges of the ears.

Tab. 2. List and definitions of the horizontal and vertical facial measurements (Mantelakis et al. 2018, 3–4)

Horizontal	**Definition**
1. Intercanthal	The horizontal distance from the left lateral canthus to the right lateral canthus.
2. Interdacryon	The horizontal distance between the eyes from the left dacryon to the right dacryon.
3. Interalae	The horizontal distance between the left lateral rims of the ala of the nose to the right lateral rim of the nose.
4. Intercheilion	The horizontal distance from the left cheilion to the cheilion of the mouth.
5. Intertemporal	The horizontal distance from the soft tissue lateral border of the left temple to the soft lateral tissue lateral border of the right temple measured along a line that passed through the estimated location of the supraorbital foramen.
6. Nose width	The horizontal measurement of the width of the nose in the region of the bony dorsum.
Vertical	Definition
Measurement 1	Trichion to the line bisecting the intertemporal line.
Measurement 2	Intereye point to soft menton.
Measurement 3	Intereye point to stomion.
Measurement 4	Intereye point to ala point.
Measurement 5	Ala point to stomion.
Measurement 6	Ala point to soft menton.
Measurement 7	Stomion to soft menton.

Almost three hundred participants in the survey evaluated the beauty of twenty female and twenty male models from photographs on a ten-point scale. On the basis of this evaluation, the authors not only pointed to those facial parameters that were distinguished in the assessed faces as the most beautiful and the least beautiful[54] (i.e. the measurements between individual facial parts that were essential for distinguishing a beautiful and a less beautiful face), but, with reference to the twelve ratios measured in both the female and male faces, the range of values (or the dispersion of the values) within which individual measurements (distances) should fall so that a face was still assessed as beautiful were identified. A comparison

54 Although photographs of models were evaluated.

of whether the identified ratio values matched the golden ratio value was among the interesting contributions. They found that only one of the twelve assessed parameters was similar to the golden ratio (the parameter of the intereye-soft menton/intereye-stomion), while all other parameters significantly differed from the value of 1.618 (Mantelakis et al. 2018).

Similar outcomes were produced by the team of Rossetti et al. (2013). In the first phase of the research the fifteen most beautiful and fifteen least beautiful faces of men and women were selected out of 400 photographs. Subsequently, several facial distances were measured using stereophotogrammetric facial reconstruction, and ten ratios were computed. The authors compared the values of these ten ratios and discovered that only three of them approached the hypothetical value of 1.618, and seven of them were significantly (statistically) different from the golden ratio. A number of other authors working within this sphere of research have even stated that the achievement of the divine proportions seems to have little, if any, influence on the overall aesthetic outcomes (Shell, Woods 2004).

3.3.1.3. Applying the Idea of the Average

Another mathematical parameter frequently used in the examination of the beauty of the human face is the average. At first glance, the average might appear as something that almost opposes beauty, as beautiful objects (works, faces, etc.) are typically exceptional and unique. However, history as well as the latest research has demonstrated the power of the influence of this variable on the beauty of the human face. One of the first research findings related to this sphere of investigation dates back to the 19th century, and is associated with the statistician, sociologist, psychologist and anthropologist, Francis Galton (1822–1911). Although Galton dealt with the issue of beauty,[55] his findings related to the effects of the calculation of an average were originally a by-product of other research. Galton sought to create a face, characteristic of a criminal, by collecting photographs of criminals. Furthermore, he subdivided them into categories to include those convicted of larceny, murder and rape (Francis 2013)

55 In Africa, he measured the figures of indigenous women (from a decent distance) and "found them impressive with those to Englishwomen" (Hunt 2007, 237). Subsequently, after his return home, he observed the beauty of local women in several English towns, of which he kept detailed records, and he uncovered the fact that London had the most frequent occurrence of beautiful women, while Aberdeen had the lowest frequency of occurrence (Hunt 2007).

hoping to find some common facial features. However, he did not measure the individual faces, but his method was to "throw faint images of several portraits, in succession, upon the same sensitised photographic plate", in order to obtain "with mechanical precision a generalised picture" (Galton 1879, 133). This resulted in the original faces with their various anomalies generating a resulting face that was more pleasing and more beautiful in appearance than most of the original faces of the criminals. Although the original intention to create an apparent prototype of the face of a criminal had already been discussed during Galton's life, the fact is that the link that he uncovered between the averageness of the human face and attractiveness was not wrong.

The effect of averageness on the perceived beauty of a human face has been confirmed by much research - a composite that combines two to four faces is more beautiful than a single face. It is even valid to say that the more faces that are blended together, the more beautiful the resulting face (Ettcoff 1999). Several facts are responsible for this phenomenon. The first is that by calculating an average the extremes and anomalies, which may occur in faces, are eliminated. Evolutionarily, such divergence is a symptom of the organism's inability to resist the negative environmental influences and is related to unhealthy mutations. Divergence is thus a reflection of developmental instability, and is an outward signal of unhealthy genes. Sexually reproductive organisms (i.e. also humans) have developed the ability to identify mutant traits through their unusual (or rare) appearance (Koeslag and Koeslag 1994). Due to an evolutionary preference for healthy and resistant organisms[56] a preference for organisms that (also through averageness) signal developmental stability has also developed. As far as human faces are concerned, this preference appears to be supported by mechanisms of positive emotional experience (feelings of pleasure, beauty, admiration, etc. for such objects) and reinforcement, as those areas of the brain responsible for the reward mechanisms are activated when perceiving beautiful faces. The outcomes of many studies point to a close relationship between the perception of beautiful faces and activity in the parts of the brain called the "brain reward systems" (see, e.g. Aharon et al. 2001; Liang, Zebrowitz, Zhang 2010; Shen et al. 2016). They include, e.g. the medial orbitofrontal cortex, the nucleus accumbens (Aharon et al. 2001) or the amygdala (Winston et al. 2007).

56 These will survive and produce healthier and more successful offspring with a higher likelihood than the organisms that are ill and easily succumb to negative influences.

Another explanation may be associated with the effect produced by average objects. An average face is a certain kind of prototype[57] of the faces that we encounter in our lives. On the basis of our experience with human faces, we create a model, a prototype, an idea of what faces should look like. This mechanism also applies to all other objects - the creation of prototypes as representatives of the classes of similar objects is a cognitive mechanism that facilitates our orientation in the world. A prototype is an artificially created picture of what we expect in association with such objects. Every other perception of an object is accompanied by a comparison of the given object with the prototype, and an evaluation of similarity or difference. Similarity or correspondence signals that the object belongs to a certain class of objects, and therefore, although as such we may perceive it for the first time, this object can be attributed with the qualities and characteristics of the objects that fall into this class without having to know the full details of this object. It greatly facilitates our orientation in the world and is associated with significant savings in time and energy. On the contrary, if the object we perceive significantly differs from the prototypes we have created, it is a signal of something that is unfamiliar - of something which may have unknown, unpredictable and potentially dangerous characteristics. It is an evolutionarily conditioned reaction, as an unknown thing or organism is a potential source of danger for humans. Analogously, a face that is different from the prototype of faces we have created is unknown; it generates care, worry, watchfulness. A person who encounters such a face does not know what can be expected from its possessor, and therefore, they are careful, tense and ready for fight or flight, if needed. Fear of the unknown or xenophobia is considered to be fundamental fears (Carleton 2016). The perception of unknown faces is mostly associated with negative feelings - they can evoke fear (Cao, Han, Hirshleifer and Zhang 2011) or hostility. On the other hand, a face that is similar or corresponds to the prototype of faces we have created generates feeling of familiarity, and the possessor will supposedly react and behave in a manner[58] that one has

57 A prototype is not an ideal, which will be discussed later. It is a characteristic representative of the given type, not its desirable form. The simplest way of creating a prototype is the calculation of the average, although typically from a very limited sample. Most frequently, a prototype is created as a primary model, i.e. before statistical evaluation (the ideal is created afterwards), and it refers to a model example in the given category, or (if it was established) to a standard whose size (shape) has been accepted as the basic parameters - a model.

58 Nowadays, it is even known that, based on experience, personal characteristics such as extroversion can be seen relatively clearly from individual facial features (Borkenau, Brecke, Möttig, Paelecke 2009), introversion (Selecká 2017), dominance (Keating, Mazur,

previously encountered. Thus, the perception of average faces is associated with positive emotions, and reflects an evolutionary mechanism which is based on a cognitive process that favours members of the prototypical category and therefore also strongly favours those faces that are close to the average of the population (Langlois, Roggman 1990).

In relation to averageness and its association with the beauty of the human face, it needs to be emphasized that averageness is not ordinariness. Although a prototype of the face is created on the basis of the experience of the perception of all the faces that we have encountered over our lives, it does not mean that a prototype of the faces is the one that we encounter most often. A mechanism that worked in this way would record the frequency with which we encounter faces, and it would choose the most frequent face.[59] However, the prototype created by human cognitive mechanisms is actually an average of all perceived faces, not a picture of the most frequently perceived face. The face created by the averaging mechanism is highly attractive, and as such, it occurs to a minimal extent in the population (Alley, Cunningham 1991). This is due to the creation of the prototype through the "artificial" mechanism of a mathematical calculation of the average, and almost every face has certain specific features that distinguish it from the prototype. The more a real face approaches such a prototype, the more beautiful it is considered.

3.3.1.4. Applying the Idea of Symmetry

Several thinkers believe that the idea of averageness leads to the idea of symmetry. The reason is that averaging should "eliminate" various factors that result in asymmetry.[60] Considering the bilateralism of the human body and face, in the case of facial symmetry we may speak of directional (a) symmetry or fluctuating asymmetry. Directional asymmetry means, in particular, differences between the right and the left halves primarily caused by the specific activity of the individual (Havlíček, Rubešová 2008, 191). It is rather evident that we are substantially more sensitive to vertical

---

Segall 1981), trustworthiness (Todorov 2008), openness to experience, agreeableness, conscientiousness, neuroticism (Little, Perrett 2007) or intelligence (Démuthová, Démuth 2016).

59 In such a case, it would be most likely be the face of our relative, which would be a self-destructive strategy from an evolutionary perspective with regard to the negative effects of inbreeding.

60 However, this is only true if we do not average highly asymmetrical individuals or provided that their asymmetry is naturally distributed.

symmetry than to horizontal symmetry (Hyllová 1976). This type of bilateral symmetry is (e.g. Gardner 1964) caused by the vertical force of gravity and the fore/aft asymmetry of the direction of motion (e.g. Gardner 1964). It is formed as a natural result of forward motion, which is proven by the greater directional asymmetry of organisms that move very slowly or do not move at all (Troje and Bülthof 1998).[61] Horizontal directional symmetry is not so important to us, mainly due to the complete absence of vertical movement and the consequent changes in our appearance. On the other hand, fluctuating asymmetry (both horizontal and vertical) appears to be important and is related to the random differences between the two halves, which we assume are formed due to inappropriate gene expression or as the result of a specific type of behaviour.

There is no doubt that symmetrical faces exhibit a substantially higher degree of attractiveness than less symmetrical ones. This is true transculturally and across various age groups.[62] Despite this, the expectation that a perfectly symmetrical face should appear more beautiful than a face with some minor deviations from symmetry is not true. A possible reason is that it is impossible to find a perfectly symmetrical face in nature. It can only be formed as the result of numerous composites or as a mirror image of the right or left half of the face. This type of perfect geometric symmetry usually appears unconvincing and artificial, and we therefore prefer highly symmetrical faces with small natural imperfections (Zaidel, Deblieck 2007). During normal perception, we never see both sides of the face in the same way, since our visual apparatus also has preferences based on the dominance of one eye or the field of view in which we perceive the object. A specific issue in the study of the importance of symmetry for the attractiveness of the human face is the question of the importance of right versus left symmetry. Research by several authors (e.g. Butler, Harvey 2005; Parente, Tommasi 2008) has found that when forming symmetrical human faces there was a substantial difference in whether the artificial face was

61 This phenomenon is related to the physical forces that act on a moving body. Symmetry is thus the consequence of the application of force (the bypassing of the surrounding environment) during movement (e.g. snail vs. a shark). On the other hand, very slow-moving organisms must be adapted for the possibility of attack by a predator from either side, and therefore they can also be very symmetrical, due to the distribution of their receptors (starfish, sea urchins etc.).

62 An intriguing yet natural fact is that as a result of tissue aging, the extent of facial asymmetry increases with age (Perrett et al. 1999), thus increasing the symmetry of older faces makes them substantially more attractive than applying the same procedure to children's faces, which are naturally more symmetrical (Kowner 1996).

formed as the mirror image of the right or the left side of the face.[63] This issue was studied in greater detail by Wolff (1933), who showed that facial samples produced through the combination of the left and mirror left of peoples' faces were thought by subjects to look more like the original people than faces produced through the combination of the right and mirror right (Burt and Perrett 1997). Later, neurological concepts that interpreted these finding emerged; according to some of them (see DeRenzi et al. 1994; Burt and Perrett 1997) the right hemisphere (which processes visual stimuli from the left part of the field of view) is in charge of the processing of facial identity, expression and facial gender. The right hemisphere is better at the analysis of the spatial configuration of any visual pattern and therefore predominates in face processing (Rhodes 1993). In addition to the older evidence from prosopagnosic patients, who had sustained damage to their right hemisphere (DeRenzi et al. 1994), more sophisticated imaging methods are now available (e.g. fMRI). The reason for such a preference may be the fact that in healthy subjects facial expressions, and in particular spontaneous smile, are larger on the left side than on the right side of the face (Borod et al. 1998; Okamoto, Haraguchi, Takada 2010), hence this (from the percipient's perspective, the left) part of the face is more important for facial perception. Current research confirms that faces created as the mirror image of the left part of the face are generally considered to be much more beautiful than the faces of the very same person formed as the mirror image of the right half (Démuthová, Selecká, Démuth 2019).[64]

The intuitively long-accepted assumption that facial or bodily symmetry represents the key attribute of attractiveness was reviewed by Nancy Etcoff and Gilian Rhodes. Rhodes et al. (Rhodes, Sumich, Byatt 1999) using perfectly symmetrical composite faces proved that even though facial attractiveness correlates with symmetry, it is not its only critical variable.[65] Similarly, in the measurement of the symmetry of attractive faces (faces which were labelled as beautiful irrespective of their symmetry), symme-

63 The "left-side" image of a face is the artificial image of a face formed from the left side of the perceived face and its mirror image. Left side of face means the left side from the percipients perspective (the one who observes the photograph/image).

64 This may be related to right-hand dominance and the mechanisms for the processing of visual stimuli. It remains unclear whether a preference for right-side mirror images would be greater than for left-side images among individuals who have the opposite dominant hemisphere (the right hemisphere dominant) than in the majority of the population. Preliminary research results do not seem to prove this is so (Démuthová, Selecká, Démuth 2019).

65 In this sense, David Perrett gives the example of the face of the young Gerard Depardieu, which despite not being particularly symmetrical is still considered to be attractive, owing to its characteristic appearance (Perrett 2010, 82).

try reached (on a scale from 1 to 10) only above-average (values 6–8) values, but not the maximum (Etcoff 1999). However, absolute facial symmetry does not guarantee its attractiveness (it may even harm it); but beautiful faces tend to possess significant symmetry.

The preference for facial symmetry tends to be accounted for through two basic types of theory. The first is a cognitive-oriented theory that assumes that preferences for symmetry lie in the processing of visual signals, which takes place simultaneously in both hemispheres. Symmetrical stimuli are therefore processed more easily and are less energy-consuming since no complex interpretation of differences has to take place. This explains the general preference for symmetrical faces in the process of perception but not in the specificities of facial perception. In fact, we know that facial perception is processed in a specific area of the cortex and that facial symmetry is perceived positively when we perceive it in its natural orientation (forehead at the top, chin at the bottom), but this preference was not observed with a horizontally rotated face (chin up) (Little, Jones 2003). The main argument for the cognitive preference of facial symmetry is the energy efficiency and processing speed (or the fact that it serves as a prototype), as well as the possibility to ignore eventually energy-demanding characteristic axial or fluctuating asymmetries while maintaining other specificities of observation (e.g. spatial orientation).

On the other hand, the evolutionary theory for the preference of facial symmetry assumes that the latter is the result of an adaptation for the selection of a genetically suitable and high-quality mate. David Ian Perrett (Perrett 2010) and many other psychologists with a similar orientation have emphasized that faces which are, from the perspective of axis and fluctuation, non-symmetrical and deformed are not usually assessed positively or paid much attention. Scientists are revealing the reasons for this preference in the evolutionary past of man and the evolutionary-based theory of probability and its calculations. It shows that the symmetry of the face or figure is a manifestation of gene intensity, which is a significant motivator of sexual behaviour - partner selection. In particular, a low level of asymmetry proves a high level of developmental stability of the organism. An organism without any signs of fluctuating asymmetry is a manifestation of the ability to cope very well with pathogens, toxins and other negative environmental factors. Symmetrical faces thus signal the appropriateness and "salubrity" of genes. Less symmetrical faces indicate hereditary[66] or

66 Hereditary malformations or individually acquired disabilities (e.g. by stroke) as a result of hereditary predispositions.

potential hereditary issues[67] associated with the bearers of the genes. The calculation of averageness, proportions and facial symmetry is thus connected with the calculation of the probability of the optimum qualities of the bearer in the fight for the highest possible probability of the successful survival of one's own genes.

3.3.1.5. Contemporary Research into Beautiful Faces

The technology of the 21st century (particularly computer modelling of the human face) has enabled the rise of new approaches to the examination of the proportions of a beautiful face. Instead of searching for and proving the presence of ideal (golden) proportions in the measurements of individual facial parts or in their mutual ratios, recent research has adopted a more comprehensive approach. The ability to scan faces (or their photographs), and to use the unlimited amounts of data from such scans in calculations has brought forth new possibilities.

An area of research has focused on uncovering the features (distances between monitored facial points, their mutual ratios or other relationships) characteristic of a beautiful face. Briefly, it dealt with the procedures for the evaluation of photographs made under standard conditions (lighting, distance, picture quality/definition, neutral facial expressions, the absence of tattoos, make-up, etc.) of many individuals, who thus provided data on the perception of beauty of such faces. Subsequently, a group with high levels of beauty as well as a group with low levels of beauty could be separated through such an evaluation. Precise calculations based on a comparison of the facial characteristics of both groups thus enabled the identification of those features[68] that it is supposed can be used to distinguish a very beautiful face from an only slightly beautiful face.

However, certain methodological deficiencies were revealed after the study of the outcomes of such research. The first major problem is the understanding of the term "beauty" itself. For example, it appeared that the use of this term offered a quite broad interpretation. The face of an old woman captured by an artist could be considered to be beautiful, because her beauty was perceived in the production of the drawing and its artis-

67 Scars, piercing or tattoo as signs of potential dangerous behaviour. (cf.: Chatterjee 2014).

68 They included symmetry (Fink, Neave, Manning, Grammer 2006), the previously mentioned averageness (Rhodes et al. 2001), the presence of secondary sexual characteristics (Hoss, Ramsey, Griffin, Langlois 2005), skin smoothness (Eisenthal, Dror, and Ruppin 2006) and skin colouration (Scott et al. 2010), etc.

tic value, the face of a model or a small child could also be considered beautiful. Therefore, in a quick and spontaneous evaluation of the human face, the term "attractiveness" has become more established, as it also includes[69] the aspect of appeal.

Another problem was that the real faces of individuals were evaluated. In such cases, the beauty evaluation might have been influenced by specific facial features that were not directly associated with the distances between the monitored points that, however, influenced the evaluation of beauty (e.g. contrast between skin and lips, skin texture or skin pigmentation, etc.). In an effort to eliminate these considerations the methods advanced to a new level, a combination with a calculation of the average. So-called facial composites were created, which served as the basis for the application of the research outcomes. In this context, a facial composite is produced by blending several faces together, which results in an "average face", created from the group of real faces. An advantage of such facial composites is that the average eliminates possible anomalies/extremes (whether in a positive or a negative sense), which can occur in any particular face. Basically, it is the creation of a form of "average" face. As opposed to the prototype, which works with all faces, a facial composite can be computed using the same mechanism from an arbitrary group of photographs (scans) of human faces.

An initial disadvantage of such a composite was that the process of composite creation through a calculation of the average of the spatial relationships between facial features also led to the smoothing out of facial features and skin texture (Rhodes 2006). This smoothing effect could artificially increase the attractiveness of the average face (Pallett, Link, Lee 2010); hence it was necessary to eliminate it. The advantages of computer-based face adjustment were used, ensuring the "normal" appearance of the skin of the facial composite.

The ability to work with facial composites resulted in a new area of research on facial attractiveness. The possibility to create composites from an arbitrary group of faces with a common specific characteristic feature opened up this branch of research. Computer-based calculations were accompanied by other data, for instance, from the field of psychometrics. In addition to photographing and scanning faces, the analyses also included measurements of psychological variables using tests, questionnaires or other methods. After the application of this approach, individual

69 From an etymological perspective, the word "attractiveness" has its roots in the Latin expression *attrahere*, which means "to draw, pull; to attract" (Harper 2018a).

faces could be grouped on the basis of the level of occurrence of a selected psychological variable (e.g. personal or performance characteristics). The mutual comparison of these groups provided the identified specific facial features, which distinguished individuals with different levels of the monitored psychological characteristics. The results included the facial composites of extroverts and introverts (Penton-Voak, Pound, Little, Perrett 2006), dominant and submissive individuals (Little, Perrett 2007) or people with high and low levels of intelligence (Kleisner, Chvátalová, Flegr 2014). The possibilities of such an approach are basically unlimited. It is interesting that the verification of the correctness of such composites proved that individual composites representing the individual (personal or other) characteristics of individuals were generally identifiable, and the given characteristics were correctly attributed to the composites. Therefore, it is obvious that what is measured by computers as characteristic differences in the faces of the groups of photographs representing high and low levels of psychological variables can be identified by people.

The link between these new approaches in facial "mathematization" and attractiveness can be used in their further work. The researchers not only created composites, but they also examined to who and under what circumstances such faces would appear attractive. It is unquestionable that it is advantageous that adjustments can be applied to the basic composite face, while the resulting computer-adjusted composites will only differ in the type of characteristics presented (the face itself will remain unchanged), or only in the extent to which they are applied to the basic composite face. Therefore, it can be said with certainty that if differences in the evaluation of the attractiveness of composites appear, they are certainly caused by the adjustments made to the composite and not by other factors.

The advantage of measuring human faces and evaluating their attractiveness, the collection of different faces and the possibility to process them within computers has also opened new possibilities in the area of their use within artificial intelligence. Due to the amount of data collected on the attractiveness of the human face, researchers sought to create programmes using such data to estimate the evaluation of the attractiveness of a human face. It showed that the level of knowledge and the amount of data available have enabled such programmes to evaluate the level of the attractiveness of a presented human face with an almost identical result as when evaluated by real people (see, e.g. Kagian et al. 2008). An example is the research conducted by Eisenthal, Dror and Ruppin (2006), in which computer software evaluated faces on the basis of forty-two criteria. The outcomes showed statistically significant correlations between the results of the evaluation of attractiveness by the computer software and the evaluation of the human assessors. Subsequently, the field of artificial intelligence can retrospectively model the possible process of evaluation followed by people, and reveal how, why and when a human face is considered to be attractive. Although it is only a partial finding relating to a specific form of the beauty of the human face, especially influenced by its significance for one's survival (i.e. with a significantly evolutionary basis), it has the potential to clarify at least a part of the mechanisms that participate in the understanding of beauty.

It is obvious from the aforementioned examples that different measurements can make parameters of beautiful faces accessible. In this context, an interesting question is the relationship between these exact mathematical measurements to the process taking place in our cognitive apparatus that results in the evaluation of a human face as beautiful. If a number of beautiful faces undergo detailed measurement and analysis, we are able, to a certain extent and also with the help of technical devices that enable many parallel calculations, to specify what parameters these faces have in common and what distinguishes them from less beautiful faces. On the basis of such knowledge, we are able to model a face that corresponds to the attributes of beauty, which will be evaluated as beautiful. However, can we consider the fact that similar procedures are applied in the actual evaluation of the beauty of a human face and that our evaluation is the result of a similar series of calculations in our brain, or are such measurements artificial and unnatural? Several concepts supporting this assumption suggest that the human cognitive apparatus actually executes such calculations (see, e.g. an earlier reflection on the existence of a "face averaging device" in perception - Symons 1979; 1995, or a later approach to the perception of beautiful faces, which understands the evaluation of attractiveness as a hidden (unconscious) algorithm of calculation - Démuth 2009a); and the current research on the attractiveness of the human face has brought results not only in the form of the objectification of beauty, but also in the form of the clarification of the processes taking place in the perception and evaluation of beauty (attractiveness) of human faces.

As with visual beauty, mathematics can be also considered to be responsible for the pleasant feelings we experience in auditory beauty. It appears that in general, we like finding patterns, sequences and motives in music that have certain rules, regularities and repetitions. We like discovering the hidden logic; we become familiar with the symmetries of songs as their essential elements. A substantial part of a beautiful song is based on such symmetric motives. An example could be the composition of Bach's repetitions and breaks. Bach frequently used repetitions of different major topics in different forms and variations. For example, a theme that composed for the French horn was used for the trumpet in its mirror form (descending-ascending), its decelerated version was used for the solo trumpet and the highly decelerated and lower-tone version of the same melody was used for the tuba, as heard in his *Contrapunctus VII.* What is specific is the fact that the beauty of all four very simple melodies only stands out when they are played together with different velocity shifts. Bach very often used this strategy (e.g. for other instruments in *Toccata and Fugue in D minor),* and it became the backbone of his music (Hofstadter 1979, Démuth 2015). The repetition of a theme, differently executed, strengthened the impression of harmony between the separate parts (as they had the same structure), as well as facilitating the identification of patterns; and it made them easier for the listener to remember. Other composers frequently used prime numbers, or Fibonacci sequence when composing their works, either purposefully or, sometimes, also unconsciously; hence the changes of motive and structure of the individual sequences that can be found in Schubert's Prelude in C, or in *Mozart's Sonata No. 1 in C Major, K.279/189d.*

All these studies have a focus on those elements, which are the objects of a certain degree of automatic and unconscious mathematical operation, in common - the calculation and comparison of observed parameters. Undoubtedly, behind these operations, there are evolutionary and cultural mechanisms and experiences based on long-term process for obtaining knowledge and the deduction of probabilities from that knowledge. While motion is associated with either danger or prey, registering attractive features is associated with an increase in the probability of success in the game of survival for one's genes and offspring. In relation to this, it is necessary to point out that the probability with which the system works is not logical, nor statistical (mathematical), but rather subjective Bayesian probability.

The mechanism by which such a form of probability functions can be explained by the following example.

3.3.2. Ideal and Composite Images

In his *Critique of Judgment,* Kant distinguished between the idea of beauty and its ideal. He considered an idea to be a rational pattern and an ideal to be a concept that fulfils this pattern, which originates from previous experiences. That means that if a Chinese man has only met women with Asian features, his ideal would be that of an average Asian face. Similarly, the ideal of a European would be represented by the average of the faces he has seen so far. Kant explains this with the example of the establishment of a standard height: "Someone has seen a thousand adult men. If he now wishes to make a judgment about their standard size, to be estimated by way of comparison, then (in our opinion) his imagination projects a large number of images (perhaps the entire thousand) onto one another. If we may be permitted to illustrate this by an analogy from optics: in the space where most of the images are united. and within the outline where the area is illuminated by the colour that is applied most heavily, the average size will emerge, equally distant in both height and breadth from the outermost bounds of the tallest and shortest in stature; and that is the stature of a beautiful man" (1975, 73). Therefore, the standard ideal originates in an unconscious mathematical calculation. The unconsciousness of it is documented not only by the aforementioned conviction of a real and consciously incomplete comparison, but also with the thought that "the same result could be obtained mechanically, by measuring the entire thousand, adding up all their separate heights and breadths (and thicknesses) by themselves and then dividing the individual sums by a thousand. And yet the imagination does exactly that by means of a dynamic effect that arises from its multiple apprehension of such shapes on the organ of inner sense" (Kant 1975, 73).

Kant's concept on the formation of ideals is remarkable in several contexts. Not only was he aware that our senses or brains perform comparisons - calculations made using all the objects of the given type perceived so far - but also that these calculations are more or less unconscious, yet it is possible to reveal their governing algorithm. This aspect connected him to the rest of the Enlightenment philosophical tradition (Reid, Hume).

The fact that Kant's deductive assumption is not only an unverifiable thought experiment but also has been confirmed through scientific research is very interesting. An example of such confirmation is Francis Galton's experiment that sought the typical features of a criminal. He discovered that a construct which originated from a compilation of individual faces and an average picture were always more attractive than any other individual face. Langlois and Roggman (1990), who carried out an experiment on the production of composite pictures using the faces of Japanese prisoners, also, much later, came to a similar conclusion. Galton actually searched for composite pictures - merging the individual pictures of the faces of criminals into one - average face.

It is interesting that the overall shape and appearance of the composite picture is especially dependent on the quantity and nature of the averaged faces. However, the composite picture quite rapidly stabilizes and its appearance basically ceases any longer to change. There is evidently a relatively great degree of similarity in the individual parameters of particular faces, despite the fact that we feel that we are different in real life. Any deviation from the stabilized composite thus becomes relatively significant. Vice versa, we have poor sensitivity in the perception of, for example, the uniqueness of racially different face types (it is more difficult to identify the faces of Asians or Africans if we lack the appropriate amount of experience), proving that our facial composite (of Asian faces in this case) is based on a relatively small sample size and thus every new face is still stabilizing it. Although its difference from the European facial composite, we have so far experienced, is still relatively significant (thus it is identified as a different face type), individually perceived faces much more resemble the Asian face composite than the alternative of potentially belonging to the European face type. Therefore, we identify a certain type difference, but it is more demanding to orient ourselves in the comparison of individual faces with this relatively new, not yet stabilized composite.[70]

Even though Kant was active in an important seaport, he worked in a geographically and racially closed world, since a relatively high degree of isolation and ethnic homogeneity was typical in the 18th century in comparison to the world of today. Therefore, his note related to the differences in the judgements of Europeans and Chinese had its own justification in the diversity of the potential visual experiences that forms our ideal. In our current, relatively globalized society, where it is possible to encounter relatively diverse visual templates either in person, or through the media, fashion and art, the production of our composite ideal is affected by greater diversity and thus it inclines to a certain more or less global composite

70 The problem of the correctness of face composite images is a relatively serious methodological issue for research into face attractiveness. Composites as such are always a construct of one's mind and do not represent a real human face. By comparing various face types, we can produce a more global composite; however, the problem is that it is less real than actual faces. This is not only related to neglecting specific features, such as colour and complexion, but also neglecting the overall appearance. The global composite as the product of merging various face types (of all ethnicities, races, manifested masculinity or femininity, etc.) deviates from the real faces that it is possible to see in world, because it diminishes the characteristic features related to gene expression. This is why numerous cognitive scientists tend to refrain from a global composite image and rather prefer "smaller" composites, which are more intrinsically coherent and generally retain certain ethnical, racial, sexual and other specifics.

image that preserves the characteristics of real faces. This is dependent on the extent, structure and amount of aesthetic experience.

It seems that the Kantian algorithm for the calculation of an ideal or standard of judgement is not mere averaging but considers the frequency of individual observations and probably also their subjective significance.

It is evident that the quantity of individual aesthetic experiences influences the formation of our ideal and, in general, taste. In the process of averaging, individual visual stimuli do not only represent items which are independent from their frequency of perception. On the contrary, the average is indeed affected by the frequency of occurrence. In other words: not every face, body or perceived object equally influences our average.[71] Far from it. Faces we perceive the most frequently have the most significantly effect in the production of the composite. That might be a reason behind the potential relevance of the Freudian attraction of a son by his mother's (or nurse's) face or a father for his daughter. The visual environment in which we live influences us not only through the structure of its elements, but also by the frequency of their occurrence. Similarly to our auditory environment - when the structure and occurrence of individual phonemes affect our sensitivity to the perception of certain sounds (e.g. if these are not typical in our auditorily stimulating environment - r/l in Japanese), through the specialization of auditory cortex we lose our potential sensitivity to the aforementioned stimuli in favour of increasing sensitivity to others (auditorily stimulated differences) - visual stimuli also forms our sensitivity to help us to distinguish what we see. Objects we often perceive form and stabilize the ideal more significantly than others. On the other hand, considering the phenomenon of habituation, it would not be appropriate to expect that each aesthetic experience is always equal, respectively, something we have seen. On the contrary, frequently perceived phenomena rapidly become boring and can result in aversion (e.g. kitsch). In relation to this, therefore, it would be highly interesting to reflect on the potential mathematization of aversion or the loss of influence by positively

71 Thus, we differentiate between arithmetic mean, weighted average, median and modus in mathematics. The arithmetic mean ignores the frequency of the representation of individual values in the given set (it is the sum of all elements, consequently divided by the quantity); the median is expressed by the middle value (dividing a series of ascending values into two numerically equal halves) and modus which is the value which occurs most frequently in the given set (the most typical feature in this sense). However, the arithmetic mean, weighted average, median and modus values may correspond or be very close, if the set is relatively large, homogeneously structured and sufficiently randomized.

perceived aesthetic experience and potential changes in its assessment associated to the relative or absolute frequency of its occurrence.

3.3.3. Taste and the Calculation of Average Values for Opinions

However important, Kant's reflections on the creation of the ideal in the creation of individual or social taste suggested that individual taste was created on the basis of personal "mathematics" with those objects perceived or imagined until to now. Based on their comparison, we create a certain personal ranking with those that saturate our aesthetic feelings evaluated as the best, and those which cause no saturation gain a negative evaluation. It is obvious that with a very limited range of a specific source of aesthetic experience (e.g. I have experience with only two types of wine), my evaluation will be very rough and have little relevance. Therefore, through the power of my own imagination, I am able through analogy to complete a continuum of the individual tastes of different wines from other experiences, and also imagine the taste of wines that I have not yet tried, but which I would likely consider to be the best on the basis of my own preferences. This can also be applied to people, clothes and architecture of possible objects. Kant followed Hume in this matter.

David Hume (Hume 2008) taught us that taste was not only the scales of experience gained so far, but it could be also considerably affected by the experience one could imagine from someone else's story. It is clear that the weight of an individual experience is also dependent on the relevance and significance of the opinion of the one with whose opinion we identify. Hume believed his critics were important in relation to this. Critics represent an authority in the formation of personal individual taste, but not only because they teach us what to refer to and how. Their importance also lies in the fact that their opinion forms and completes the experience of individuals who have not yet directly experienced it, thus framing a richer, i.e. more relevant continuum. According to Hume, however, the authority of critics lies not only in their greater experience (an opinion of the more experienced individual as one who has perceived more appears to be more relevant than the opinion of a less experienced individual), but also in their greater sensitivity and erudition (they know what to examine, they have studied a lot - 2008). Therefore, it happens that on the basis of someone else's experience I design my own range of aesthetic experience and evaluation, also reflecting the objects that fill my empty spaces (I have not experienced them directly) also with provisionally accepted evaluations. The criterion that justifies the acceptance of relevant evaluations of individual critics or evaluators who have significance for us (mother, father, husband, friend, etc.) is mostly whether we actually identify with the given evaluation or not in the subsequent direct experience with a preliminarily classified and evaluated object. As long as the aesthetic judgements of a critic have not been approved in the individual experience of a majority of individuals, the critic is no longer an authority, and vice versa. Kant and Hume thus suggested that individual taste was based on comparison and the internal (statistical, Bayesian?) mathematics of experience gained or imagined to now.

A crucial feature of Hume's philosophy is its intersubjectivity. Hume approaches an aesthetic (taste-based) judgement as a social interaction (Jones 2011, 433). This also applies to Kant. He points to the fact that our aesthetic judgement does not just produce an expression of what we like, regardless of others. Taste, as long as it fulfils the demands of pure aesthetic judgement, produces more - certain objectivity, or even more - a general and inevitable validity. If I claim that something is beautiful I not only display my liking for it, but also the assumption that it is liked, or will be liked, by others. How is this possible, if taste is formed on the basis of individual and subjective experience?

The heart of the problem with fashion or taste as a social phenomenon is in the fact that it is also created as an individual ideal or an individual taste. When forming social taste, a composite image is made, or an average value is calculated of how individual subjective rankings and evaluations are overlaid. Fashion or social aesthetic standards are therefore nothing more than average values calculated in time and space, i.e. a composite of individual tastes.

Certainly, it is possible to object that actual taste differs from fashion or common, most frequently formed aesthetic judgements. Art critics display an ability to distinguish between high and low, extraordinary and ordinary. They typically do not perceive the mainstream as taste, but as its considerable simplification (or even gaudiness). After all, beauty is not what we perceive as average, but exceptional. But beware! Notwithstanding all these reflections on averageness and composite images, beauty has not been said to lie in the average. Quite the opposite.

Beauty as an expression of aesthetic evaluation is something exclusive, unusual and rare. It is an expression of the excellence of quality, not mediocrity. However, this does not mean that it is not related to averageness (not mediocrity).[72]

---

72 The difference between mediocrity and averageness can be compared to the difference

If we have dealt with averageness so far, we have referred to symmetry, the absence of anomalies and perfection produced by balance and harmony. An average face does not exhibit particular extravagance, specific features or anomalies. Quite the opposite – it conceals them. On the other hand, it needs to be said that one cannot find a completely average face anywhere in the world. It is a rational or visual concept. This makes it rare, exceptional and exclusive. A beautiful face displays a certain averageness, yet its occurrence is unique, and if not impossible, at least rare. This exclusive and unique character makes it highly exceptional and attractive.

Similarly, the most valued experience is not average, but above-average, which is therefore exclusive to us. Group or common taste thus expresses an average of the individual tastes, but not an average as an arithmetic mean, but rather averageness. Individual eccentric elements and anomalies are eliminated, and the relativity of individual tastes thus ultimately produces the objectivity of the accord. However, this is not an average. It is uninteresting. What we seek to uncover is what is perceived as above-average in the majority of subjective aesthetic judgements.

The issue of exclusiveness and non-mediocrity of the aesthetic judgement of an expert as opposed to a common sense judgement is an old problem in aesthetic judgement. The best critic is said to be able to distinguish between different aesthetic objects, and to determine what is beautiful, independent of the opinions of others. Their judgement in relation to beauty is absolute "as such", outside of the space-time continuum. It is an expression of the objective qualities of an object, not an expression of the opinions of a community. Such a "Platonic" critic will mostly stand alone, will go against the mainstream and their judgement will be timeless.

In contrast stands an expert who realizes that their judgement will be an expression of the time and community in which they live. However, as long as they present the average they will not be experts, but rather ordi-

between arithmetic and weighted means. An arithmetic mean represents a statistical concept that expresses the typical value of the given set. Its value is the sum of the values of all the components divided by the number of components. Arithmetic mean is thus very likely to be deformed by extreme values. On the contrary, a weighted mean is a form of arithmetic mean that reflects the varying importance (weights) of individual values. It is used to calculate the overall arithmetic mean of a set that comprises several subsets (e.g. the evaluation of the value of a parameter such as size and the level of its attractiveness). From the perspective of averageness, it is an expression of two different concepts – arithmetic mean reflecting the extent of the representation of individual components, and an expression of their values from the perspective of attractiveness. Averageness expresses mediocrity from the viewpoint of the representation of components regardless of their attractiveness, as well as absolute non-mediocrity from the perspective of their aesthetic attractiveness.

nary assessors. What makes them experts is their ability to see more and better than others in a manner that makes others identify with their views, as their judgements, predictions or evaluations have proved to be reasonable. An expert, whose judgements have not been accepted by the majority, or at least a majority of the expert community, is simply not considered to be an expert in the long term. In other words: if what they express does not lead to agreement, and if their views are incompatible with the majority, they will not be accepted as experts. Similarly, if the opinion of the experts does not express a possible consensus with the public, the public ceases to accept or consider the opinion of such "experts" as relevant.[73] This returns us to the fact that the opinion of an expert or critic might not be typical of the particular time or community, yet their authority as an expert is based on the acceptance or rejection of their views. This also applies to the Platonic critic. After all, the fact that he is correct has to be seen and accepted by someone. If he really is correct, everybody will see it.

The creation of taste is thus an intersubjective activity that not only refers to the fact that our evaluations of individual perceptions are frequently affected by the evaluations of others, but also by the fact that they are made using language.

Experts have to express their aesthetic judgements in a comprehensible manner, expressing what all others might feel, or even should feel. This might not be at all easy, as subjective content such as beauty and many other aesthetic emotions or feelings are to be expressed. Not only because our language may be too poor to express the different stages of the intensity of pleasure in individual aesthetic experiences (we have more feelings than words), but especially regarding their content. Natural beauty is different from the beauty of a loving look from a partner, or a trusting look from a child. Emotions involved in different aesthetic experiences that are incited by different objects or contexts cause serious difficulties in our ability to intersubjectively convey aesthetic experience. Especially if the different aspects or qualities are observed in a single object.

Experts communicating their feelings, evaluations or predictions thus also have to deal with mathematics from a semantic perspective. They look for words that best express the semantic aspect of their feelings, the considered continuum on the evaluation scale as well as the dominant aspects and dimensions of their feelings. Mostly they do this by comparing the meanings of words to what is meant, and the level of overlap (the search

---

73 Completely empty galleries do not prove the good taste of the curator, although a full stadium does not necessarily guarantee valuable art (and mostly does not).

for concise words and comparisons), and possible analogies or metaphors, if words cannot sufficiently convey what they want to express. On the other hand, however, they also have to work with a certain likelihood of comprehensibility, i.e. with an estimation of the obviousness of their feelings and the possible overlap with the feelings of their percipients. Their message would be completely useless without this intersubjective calculation of the adequate or sufficient overlap of the mental positions of experts and percipients.

Here, we deem it important to distinguish taste, aesthetic judgement and the experience of aesthetic beauty from other aesthetic values, which can be the subject of expert aesthetic evaluation. Until now, beauty and feelings of pleasure in particular - fancy (liking) were considered (based on Kant) to be the basis of aesthetic experience. However, experts in art or aesthetes do not only have to formulate their aesthetic judgements with regard to whether they like the given object or not. And mostly they do not do so. Frequently they are able to recognize what they do not like, but which they identify as something that otherwise has aesthetic value. Whether due to its originality, elaboration, processing technology, etc. For instance, we might not like Picasso's paintings, nevertheless we perceive them as aesthetically valuable. The reason is that we do not like their sensory effects, but rather we like something else, for instance, their intellectual value. And this is the heart of the whole problem.

3.3.4. Aesthetic Value and the Calculation of Rewards

Anjan Chatterjee (2004) and some other thinkers avoid using biological and evolutionary reasonable explanations for all of the different types of beauty and aesthetic judgement. Therefore, they distinguish between hot (increasing desire) beauty and cold (calm or even meditative) beauty. While the mechanisms of evolutionary calculation can be applied to exiting beauty, cold beauty appears to be beyond such a simple explanation. However, as we believe, it only appears this way at first sight.

The mechanisms of computations and calculations, harmonies, synergies, synchronicities, etc. can even be found in the greatest and most magnificent art. Music is a good example of such a kind of art. In music, we anticipate the upcoming tones, melody and rhythm from the preceding characteristics and structure of the music that we are listening to. We do so on the basis of several factors we perceive, even when listening to entirely new songs, that we have not previously heard (Démuth 2019a).

The basis of our perception of music is the recognition of backbone elements and sequences. These create certain patterns, which we identify in music that distinguish music from disorganized noise. Further fundamental patterns and wholes that can be perceived as key (melody, rhythm) or supplementary can be recognized within such fundamental elements. From their logic, the most likely patterns for further possible development are subsequently deduced, or anticipated. Thus, listening to music is principally a mathematical operation[74] in a number of ways.[75] The first is the comparison of the pitch of tones and their mutual relationships. It is obvious that some tones go together better than others, because they have smoother ratios. An ideal ratio is represented by the rationally quantifiable multiples of the pitches (frequencies) of separate tones. For example, the use of chromatic sequence (halftones) presupposes the continuation of halftones - ala Liszt or Gershwin - contrary to the scale sequence. The harmony of such tones is called consonance, and the pair of preceding tones

74 W. G. Leibniz was convinced that "Even the pleasures of the senses are reducible to intellectual pleasures, known confusedly".

75 Mathematicians, musicians as well as cognitive scientists assume a positive correlation between the development of musical education, experience and mathematical abilities and vice versa. It was assumed that listening to classical music improved a childs intelligence as early as the prenatal period. Discussion on the issue of the correlation between intelligence and music was initiated by a study that documented the so-called *Mozart effect*, i.e. the achievement of better results after short-term stimulation with classical (Mozart's) music (Steele et al. 1999, Jausovec, Habe 2003, Jausovec et al. 2006, Jausovec, Habe 2004, Dastgheib et al. 2014). Frances H. Rauscher, Gordon L. Shaw and Catherine N. Ky performed an experiment, in which a group of university students listened to ten minutes of Mozart's *Sonata for Two Pianos in D Major, K. 448*, and then were subsequently asked to carry out spatial-intelligence tasks. It showed that listening to the given composition had positive effects on their performance (spatial IQ before and after the test, plus comparison with a control group listening to relaxing music), which led them to postulate a thesis on the so-called *Mozart effect*. Later studies confirmed that the given effect was not only generated by Mozart's music, but basically by almost any music (the *Blur effect*, named after a British band whose music led to similar outcomes). This raises the question of to what extent the improved score is a matter of composition structure, and to what extent it is a matter of a change in the rhythm of thinking and action, which are associated with music. Sylvian Moreno et al. examined the effects of musical training on an increase in verbal intelligence among three-year-old and four-year-old children. They uncovered a significant improvement in verbal intelligence recorded for those children who had attended an interactive computerized training program for music developed for preschool children after as few as 20 days of training (2011, 1425). The children who attended a similar programme of the same length focused on visual art did not show such an improvement. Similar outcomes were produced by Franziska Degé (Degé et al. 2011), whose study confirmed the positive correlations between musical training and the intelligence executive functions of 9-12-year-old children. However, the significant impact of individual music styles on intelligence, or, vice versa, correlations between intelligence and a preference for a specific type of music were not recorded (Démuth, Rušinová 2019).

helps us to logically anticipate their possible continuation. Beethoven, for example, in his *Moonlight Sonata,* immediately uses four triplets (tone triplets) in the same tonal structure at the beginning. Thus, he created a very simple but elegant melody full of consonance, which is easily anticipated and remembered.

Another essential factor of musical calculation is the distribution of tones over time.[76] The continuation of the same rhythm and melody may be deduced and anticipated from the structure of what was previously heard. Out of a plethora of possible scenarios for the possible continuation of a composition, the scenario that results from the sequence logic of what has already been heard is considered to be the most likely. No change in the rhythms or melody is expected, as it would be unlikely and energy intensive. However, sometimes a change is expected. This occurs with regard to the structure of the music, if for example the monothematic character of a composition and its rhythm is tiring, or causes an increase in tension.

The third level of calculation is the expectation of the colour of the tones and other non-fundamental moments. We would probably be very surprised, if the voices and tones that are completely different from those we have heard until now suddenly rang out. Thus, in the fragments of the facts perceived, we seek rules, according to which, we may safely anticipate the near future. Listening to music is thus an intellectual mathematical puzzle, in which, on the basis of the most likely harmonies, symmetries and tendencies, we expect a certain succession of tones, rhythms and musical sequences, and, at the same time, we are immediately confronted with the results, with the correctness or incorrectness of our predictions. If the anticipated sequence, the perceived melody or its execution appears, the music overwhelms us with a certain intellectual satisfaction. It can manifest as intellectual liking, satisfaction as well as a bodily reaction, such as

76 "Everything that emits a sound contains a vibration or a transverse motion such as we see in strings; thus everything that emits sounds gives off invisible impulses. When these are not confused, but proceed together in order but with a certain variation, they are pleasing; in the same way, we also notice certain changes from long to short syllables, and a coincidence of rhymes in poetry, which contain a silent music, as it were, and when correctly constructed are pleasant even without being sung. Drum beats, the beat and cadence of the dance, and other motions of this kind in measure and rule derive their pleasurableness from their order, for all order is an aid to the emotions. And a regular though invisible order is found also in the artfully created beats and motions of vibrating strings, pipes, bells, and indeed, even of the air itself, which these bring into uniform motion. Through our hearing, this creates a sympathetic echo in us, to which our animal spirits respond. This is why music is so well adapted to move our minds, even though this main purpose is not usually sufficiently noticed or sought after" (Leibniz 1690–1698, 425ff).

shivering (Seok 2019). It is due to the fact that the brain perceives sensory data from the surrounding world as meaningful, and confirms our ability to read them, i.e. to actively and successfully integrate them in our environment (Schoeler 2015). Aesthetic satisfaction increases as a result of the decrease of tension from the solution of intellectual issues (Huron 2006; Huron, Margulis 2010; Ignacio 2016; Koelsch, Fritz, Schlaug 2008; Müller, Klein, Jacobsen 2011; Pearce, Wiggins 2012; Salimpoor et al. 2011; Steinbeis, Koelsch, Sloboda 2006; Vuust, Kringelbach 2010). From an evolutionary perspective, it is basically an intellectual version of the biological and psychological reaction in seeking to cope with possible changes and new impulses in the environment. If we manage to do so, we know that we are ready to recognize problems in the auditory environment, and are able to handle them.

As we enjoy being able to anticipate the regularities and patterns of future musical development, we also sometimes like, if our anticipation fails us and we are pleasantly surprised by a composition. If we were able to precisely anticipate everything, the composition would be boring and of no interest. Therefore, despite the subjectively anticipated likelihood of its development, we encounter totally unexpected solutions, which show us new, equally meaningful or even better patterns and regularities of the musical puzzle. Typically, this happens in situations where the new solution is only appreciated after we have recognized the logic of the unexpected continuation, and we feel that it is correct. Post factum, we develop a new logic, we identify with new perspectives of the perception of the music, thus gaining new knowledge and a new algorithm, which can be used in the future. The author of the composition has surprised us, but our understanding of their intentions and structure revealed new possible combinational scenarios to us, which retrospectively confirm our own intellectual capacity and ability to solve the given problem.

A similar thing applies to dancing, where we not only calculate the future development of the song, but also the synchronization of the music and movements of our body, or that of another person (people) so that we create a harmonious and meaningful whole.

Certainly, one could object that we do not calculate when listening to music or dancing, but rather we intuitively feel in a special way. However, we assume that what we call intuition so frequently and vaguely is nothing than an unconscious calculation, or a calculation with unclear solution algorithm (Démuth 2009a). How this algorithm is developed and whether it is inherent (e.g. evolutionarily), or acquired through day-to-day unique experiences and its inclusion with other experiences we have had, would be the subject for separate research. Feelings, as we have sought to indicate, might be considered as the somatic response of an organism to the overall evaluation of individual inputs in the form of a global calculation (Démuth 2019b).

Some thinkers avoid reflection on the perception of, e.g. abstract works of art in a similar way. They admit that when we perceive an abstract painting, we create a complex image of the given object, which comprises the individual parts and a calculation of the most likely semantic units, but the cognitive aspect is represented totally differently in the given feelings. While "hot beauty" encodes the cognitive information indirectly in the perceived phenomenon, resulting in an increase of feelings of love and desire, cold beauty lacks desire. When we view abstract paintings, fractals, or when we meditate, the subject of our perception is mostly something complex, whose clear meaning can only be divined with difficulty. Similar factors apply to conceptual art, architecture and other forms of art. The purpose of "hot beauty" appears to be evolutionarily programmed, and our sensory system, in its evolutionary development, has developed a higher level of sensitivity to its presence, which is presented through desire. In opposition, the purpose seems to have absolutely no importance for "cold beauty". We do not like things for something, but artistic objects hold their value within themselves, within their existence, structure or simply in their being. Contrary to objects of evolutionarily acquired "hot beauty", where "cold beauty" is concerned, we might not even know precisely what and why we like something, or the sources of the beauty are perceived less clearly and without the involvement of our will. "Cold beauty" thus resembles fancy without purpose, as required by Kant, without personal involvement; or an unbiased assessment of something in relation to which we are "evolutionarily free". However, this is not entirely true.

As numerous neuro-aesthetic surveys have shown, both hot and cold beauties are associated with activity in the same neuroanatomical structures in our brains. Semir Zeki et al. proved that the sensory perception of beauty (such as the perception of faces, landscapes, etc.) was accompanied by activity in the same areas of the brain as when we perceive complex and abstract mathematical objects we consider to be beautiful. "Previous brain studies depicting the neurobiology of beauty showed that the experience of visual (Kawabata, Zeki 2004), musical (Blood et al. 1999; Ishizu and Zeki 2011) and moral (Tsukiura, Cabeza 2011) beauty correlated with activity in a specific area of the emotional brain, the area of the A1 medial-orbital-frontal cortex, which probably includes the Brodman Area (BA) segments 10, 12 and 32 (Ishizu, Zeki 2011). The results showed that experience of mathematical beauty parametrically correlated with activity in the same area of the emotional brain, namely the A1 medial orbital-frontal cortex (mOFC), as experiences of beauty derived from other sources" (Zeki et al. 2014). Moreover, not only is the feeling or assessment of beauty associated, independently of its source, with activity in the same area of the brain, it is even associated with a certain prediction of present and future pleasures.

The nucleus accumbens plays a special role in the process of anticipation of pleasure. When we perceive something we like, the limbic system, which is part of the phylogenetically oldest part of the brain – its emotional part – produces dopamine, which enables us to experience pleasure and pleasant feelings. Dopamine is produced in the ventral tegmental area, but it is released as part of the activity of the nucleus accumbens. The function of the nucleus accumbens has been long believed to be associated with the experience of pleasure and delight. However, Salimpoor's (Salimpoor 2011) research indicated that "dopamine plays an important role in the anticipation of reward, in motivating the activity, or the reward system and the decision processes that lead to the optimisation of possible benefits (Sharot et al. 2009). The function of dopamine is thus not only associated with the experience of pleasure, but especially with its anticipation" (Démuth 2018b). In other words, our brains, on the basis of experience that is either evolutionary programmed or gained through personal lessons and social communication, releases dopamine, when confronted with signals it interprets as the promise of future significant pleasure, independent of whether the objects concerned are aesthetic, ethical or mathematical. The system of rewards thus encourages behaviour it believes is suitable and profitable for the subject. It clarifies the fact that we "like" aesthetic objects, morally good behaviour or an elegant mathematical proof. Not only figuratively, but also literally.

The pleasure we experience when we evaluate aesthetically impressive objects is to a certain extent the same as the pleasure we experience when we evaluate morally good behaviour, or a scientifically excellent observation. Zeki et al. demonstrated that despite the diversity of sources and dimensions of evaluation, the same type of beautiful experience gained from art, science or morality were produced by activity in a single brain structure, through the release of dopamine from the nucleus accumbens. It proves that beautiful objects, as well as good behaviour or knowledge are promises of future pleasure. The pleasure from this kind of experience resembles the intellectual pleasure of the solution of an intellectual problem. According to the research of Tik et al. (2018), it also activates the reward system and the nucleus accumbens, which releases dopamine as a reward for solving the problem.

What we are suggesting, in this complicated way, is a basic heretical thesis that aesthetic perception is, in a certain way, the solution to an intellectual puzzle - a calculation - whether of the most likely meaning (what the given object represents), or other aspects of its appearance.

Natural beautiful objects enthuse us with their evolutionary objective, which we unconsciously perceive. Morally valuable actions are pleasing, because we understand the long-term social benefits that result from this kind of behaviour (Démuth 2019a). Intelligence and wisdom are perceived as "sexy", because living with it brings a potentially higher sum of benefits than average or stupid behaviour (Démuth, Démuthová 2018). Similar to the art that we do not like as sensory beauty, but which we appreciate intellectually. Many works of art receive our admiration and respect for their originality, others for their elaboration, the context in which they were created or new and impressive processing techniques, etc. Therefore, what we "like" about them is their elaboration, the algorithms of technical processing, the ways of depiction or the expression of ideas. And these can also be used repeatedly for other subjects and objects. This is what artists are taught in schools, studios and by their teachers. Every artist - painter - acquires the processes, worldviews and methods of depiction that they believe are valuable and will bring them success, riches and admiration. They assume that what they like will also be pleasing to others. And even if it is not, work on new processes, even at the price of misunderstanding and lack of popularity, will be compensated by other future benefits, which will bring satisfaction to the artist. Or, vice versa, if they paint something that does not enthuse them, or in a way that they do not consider to be exciting or appropriate, they are likely to do so only because this provides other (such as financial) forms of satisfaction.

3.4. Preliminary Summary

In the presented text, we sought to demonstrate that aesthetic perception (e.g. of a painting) may be understood as a quite complex process of calculation at several levels. The first one is the interpretation of the perception itself and the perception process through mathematical concepts and ideas, and perceptual calculations. What we see is what our sensory apparatus (including the brain) evaluates on the basis of mechanisms either acquired evolutionarily (inherent) or through learning (soft). The perception processes themselves are processes of multilevel comparison, evaluation and synthesis of the given data in the most probable whole.

The second level of calculations is the creation of an ideal, of both personal and social taste. We demonstrated that taste was principally an interexperience concept of the average. First of all, a concept framed on the basis of the calculation of the average values of one's own experience. In society, social taste is thus framed on the basis of intersubjective calculation of the average of individual rankings and preferences.

And, ultimately, aesthetic judgement can be considered in terms of the Bayesian theory of conditional probability. Fancy can be then perceived as a means to encourage interest in an object, form of behaviour or knowledge, with which we are convinced that their owner or the subject working with them will receive a greater degree of benefit in the future, i.e. that they are beneficial in the long term. The support of this subjectively acquired and influenced likelihood is therefore strengthened by pleasant feelings of fancy, and evaluation using the reward systems in our brain. Thus, its causes are principally purposeful.

4. Philosophical Questions Associated with the Mathematics of Beauty

All of the three aforementioned levels of understanding of aesthetic perception as a calculation not only open up room for the mathematical examination of the individual mechanisms and laws of perception or social phenomena, whose mapping, as we believe, will be further expanded, but also for the issue of our perception of reality, and the relation between reality and mathematics. Some thinkers, such as Roger Penrose (Penrose 1997), believe that the world was created according to mathematical principles, which are rooted in its deepest foundations. According to some, these principles are completely independent of the human mind, and according to Penrose, they even existed before the creation of the material world we know today. They are the codes of God, Demiurge, et al. his plans or simply principles and ideas that are valid independently of the existence of matter, which observes them. They are eternal and unchangeable. Logical, mathematical and physical laws are the principles upon which the world was created, and they are therefore incorporated in it. The role of science is their thorough revelation and also the logical and mathematical principles of our perception and cognition.

Karl Raimund Popper adopts a similar approach (Popper 1984). However, he assumes that mathematical laws exist not only in world No. 1, i.e. independent of our mind and existence, directly in the material world whose backbone they represent, but also in world No. 3, i.e. in the world of ideas which are the creations of human thinking. Mathematics, like other sciences and their ideas, is a product of human thought and, as such, it depends on it. But as far as the dependence of mathematical ideas on thinking is concerned, Popper presents a very remarkable thesis on the dependence between ideas and thinking as to their creation, as well as a certain level of independence between discoveries, inventions and ideas and their further existence. This inconsistency of dependence might appear to be a mistake in Popper's thinking. However, Popper does not claim that the given thought, idea or mathematical law exists on its own, independent of any medium. He only states that it exists independently of the mind of the person who discovered or formulated it, not only in the minds of their followers (such as memes - non-genetic replicators), but in any form in which it might be preserved. It means that, for instance, mathematical discoveries may remain untouched in the form of records, for example, for many thousands of years, and if they are later rediscovered, they will once again be expounded independently of their original author. However, it does not necessarily mean that the discoverer has to be another human. It could be an artificial intelligence, which would "understand" the given text, or be able to reproduce it. Bach's cantata or Pythagorean theorem are nowadays independent of their creators, and they exist in the world of ideas, although it is clear that they exist for someone who is able to see this world.

In contrast, there is an influential philosophical tradition that assumes that mathematical relationships, ideas and principles have been introduced into the world by us. The world is not mathematical or non-mathematical, yet our mind tends to explore it in this way, and thinking mathematically is only one of many possible approaches to the interpretation of the world and our knowledge of it. Mathematical principles of thought are not applied to us and the world because they are the actual essence of how we act, but simply because they are very convincing and efficient. Beauty is similar.

4.1. The Metaphysical Status of Beauty[77]

Thinkers of antiquity (the supporters of Pythagoreanism, Plato, etc.), as well as many medieval and modern thinkers believed that beauty was an objective quality of ideas and things, of their own characteristics and was independent of the subject who perceived them. This was also the view of Thomas Reid, who believed in beauty as an objective quality of the forms of things and to support his statement, he also referred to the affirmative character of the language, which claimed that things were or were not beautiful, not that they only appeared to be (Reid 1969). Aesthetic realism is among the most classical of approaches, but while there is a relatively wide concord and binding nature in the area of knowledge (e.g. of mathematical facts and laws) despite different geographic, cultural, historical or personality bases,[78] such concord has not been visible in the validity and binding nature of aesthetic judgements. Aesthetic judgements and evaluations appear to be significantly more sensitive to contemporary, geographic and other determinants; and their "metaphysics" may therefore be different.

A considerable proportion of modern philosophers have succumbed to the temptation to rank aesthetic experience and judgements among the secondary qualities introduced by Locke. The result of this was the idea that taste does not concern the evaluation of the objects themselves, but

77 More on the differences in the metaphysical perception of beauty in Enlightenment philosophy can be found in Démuth (2016), Démuth, Démuthová (2019).

78 2+2 equals 4 in Amazonia as well as in Zurich, in the era of Euclid as well as today.

rather the evaluation of our perceptions and impulses. Beauty, in a similar way to taste, colour or other qualities, is then only an expression of our reflection of our own ideas; and therefore, a general validity and binding nature of aesthetic judgements cannot be reasonably enforced on such a subjective basis. Beauty, in a similar way as symmetry or balance, is then only an idea and as such it does not express the objective reality of things, but only the way in which we perceive or comprehend them. George Berkeley brought this form of reflections to its full consequences, and he attributed the same ideal character to mathematical objects. He claimed they were abstract, and the only particular mathematical shapes that could be perceived were individual patterns drawn in notebooks or drawings, and geometry as a science only dealt with abstract concepts (Berkeley 2003, 13).

Contrary to beauty or grace, mathematical theorems and ideas, although ideal abstract concepts, claim objective validity. The reasons for this were sought by David Hume and Immanuel Kant. Both these enlightened thinkers concluded that objective validity and the possibility of an inevitable binding nature of scientific truths were our inputs into the world in the form of our way of thinking. The mathematical qualities of the world are thus not the qualities of things as such, but rather they represent a form of our reflections of them, and therefore, thinking about them beyond the framework of human, or rather a rational view and consideration is meaningless. However, the epistemological scepticism of Kant and Hume did not completely reject the existence of mathematical laws in the world of things as such. What they rejected was only their perceptibility beyond the framework of human thinking. And according to Ockham's rule of the economy of thought: if there is no way to enter the world of things beyond our way of thinking and perception, and thus to verify the possible existence or non-existence of such laws, there is no point in assuming certain laws beyond possible experience, as such knowledge is simply inaccessible to us. Mathematics therefore needs to be situated in the world of phenomena - the world of our thoughts. And although Kant and Hume disagreed as to the level of the binding nature of mathematical facts[79] or their sources, they found agreement as to their objective validity and ideal character. Beauty is similar. As for mathematics, both thinkers included relatively few factors that enter into the process of the evaluation of beauty, ensuring a relative-

79 Hume's *Relation between Ideas* (where mathematics and logic are included) do not have to be necessarily valid due to his asocianist view of teaching in his early philosophical opinions (*Treates*), while Kant assumed inevitable validity of Euclid's geometry and mathematics, directly guaranteed by the intrinsic forms of perception.

ly extensive and indisputable agreement between its users; however, the issue of the perception of beauty was viewed in greater complexity by both thinkers, and therefore, in the overall calculations of the level of attractiveness or pleasure, people frequently arrive at different conclusions, as they reflect many partial and differing inputs, and, especially, they do not have all the relevant experience and knowledge that might lead to a more objective calculation. In other words: Kant believed that if an agreement as to mathematical facts could be reached (with minor exceptions) in Mathematics, it could also be reached in ethics and morals, if we sufficiently frequently and thoroughly refined our ethical feeling and moral decision-making. However, it does not happen often, and even though a relatively wide unity is reached through compulsory education, such an achievement has not been recorded in ethics, which could claim general validity and a universally binding nature, because we do not practice our practical reasoning sufficiently frequently and thoroughly. Similarly, yet to an even greater extent, we do not practice our aesthetic feeling - reflecting judgement; and therefore, we do not formulate generally binding aesthetic judgements and evaluations, although as rational beings, we quite clearly often assume them (the assertoric language form of aesthetic judgements is an example). At the same time, however, we also assume the multi-factor character of individual inputs that affect our aesthetic assessment, e.g. era, cultural contexts, gained experience, temperament, etc.

4.2. Why Do We Mathematicize?

A truly serious question in aesthetic thinking is not the existence of disagreement, i.e. the inability to generally and inevitably agree on issues; but exactly the opposite - the occasional existence of agreement, or the possibility of its expectation or a claim of agreement. What surprised philosophers after Kant was the idea that if rationality, spaciousness, succession or, for example, causality were our inputs into the world in the form in which we think and perceive, how was it even possible that the world, or the phenomena in it, were actually governed by these principles, or that our forms of thinking actually "fitted" to the world as perfectly as possible in exact sciences (such as Mathematics or Physics). How could the world of phenomena be governed by the logic of our perception and judgement, or how is it possible that it is actually governed by these principles?

The answer to this question was found in philosophy after Kant; the philosophical answer to this question was found in different forms, and its roots could already be discovered in Kant's later works. Karl Raimund Popper, for instance, pointed to the fact that the agreement of mathematical, logical and scientific truths with the world was not as significant as it might appear at first glance. Popper considered scientific knowledge to have the form of theories, models and hypotheses, i.e. a form of ideas that does not always correspond to the world, or that did not always fully govern the world. What is essential is the fact that only those theories and models that have been proven to probably be true through scientific testing, i.e. the theories and models whose predictions are in accord with observations and facts in the world of phenomena, are mostly preserved in science. In other words: the models, hypotheses, theories and ideas that do not correspond to reality are generally not preserved in science, and are forgotten in the history of scientific thinking. What remains is what actually works, or vice versa: what expresses the arrangement of empirical experience in the world of phenomena is ultimately also established in science as a meaningful and reasonable theory. The world is thus not governed by theories, but theories are the concepts we use to interpret the world.

As for Mathematics, it can be assumed that it is a product of the human way of thinking, which has been very well verified over time (by its improvement and the elimination of mistakes). It is indisputable that historically several different types of "Mathematics" have existed, some of which turned out to be wrong, while others were very laborious, or not exact but only approximate, etc. Thus, one can find different forms of notation for numbers (Barrow 2002) and mathematical operations, different types of calculations (e.g. Leibniz's and Newton's infinitesimal calculus) as well as other totally incorrect convictions and theories in the history of mathematical thinking (e.g. the Pythagorean conviction that all numbers could be only expressed as a ratio of two integers). Over time, some turn out not to be the only possibility (e.g. Euclidian, respectively Lobachevsky's and Minkowski's geometry), and totally different and new types of numbers, geometries and Mathematics appear. Others turn out to be completely wrong in the first steps of their initial testing.

Contrary to the natural sciences, mathematical facts and statements are not based on sensual observation, experiment, opinion or the extent of gained experience. Their "veracity" comes rather from a convincing reasonable demonstration of the fact that a theorem necessarily results, from a logical and/or mathematical perspective, from the accepted assumptions (axioms) and statements whose validity is mostly undisputed

(Démuth 2013b). A logically inevitable nexus and a deductive system of derivation thus provides us with the feeling of the strongest level of persuasion and the most definite verification of the truth of a theorem. Reason encourages us to believe not only in the fact that something is as characterized by a mathematical proof, but also in the fact that it cannot be otherwise (Démuth 2013b). With regard to the fact that observations, or expensive and time-consuming experiments are not necessary to uncover mathematical truths, the validity or invalidity of individual mathematical theorems can be relatively easily verified. It is enough to be able to thoroughly derive the particular consequences through deductive thinking, thus verifying the validity or invalidity of the given theorems. This, along with a broad consensus (Garnier, Taylor 1996) that results from the common process of derivation using the same axioms (which always brings us to the same common conclusions, if we do not make mistakes), has caused a considerable portion of mathematicians to reject the conviction that mathematical objects, truths and ideas are only our concepts, but due to their universal validity and necessity, they believe in the autonomy of their existence and that we discover them rather than construct them. This frequently brings them to the purely Platonic perception of mathematical objects.

The issue of universal validity and the necessary binding nature of logical and mathematical judgements for rational beings can also be interpreted by approaches other than the Platonic approach. Kant, in his *Critique of Pure Reason,* clearly suggested that the general binding nature of geometric truths and arithmetic sequences lies in the intrinsic forms of our thinking, in this case in the intrinsic forms of our perception of space and time (1977). In other words: mathematical truths are very convincing, because they cannot be ignored, and we cannot think otherwise.

However, the question of why we think as we think still remains and why this way of thinking appears to be so highly effective and valid. Friedrich Wilhelm Joseph von Schelling offered an interesting answer to the Kantian question of why our forms of perception and thought were in accord with the forms in which the world is arranged. Schelling was convinced that the forms of our rationality are the result of the long-term process of the objectivization of rationality in nature, i.e. that our forms of thought were in accord with nature, as they were ultimately the natural forms of thought, or the forms of thought in nature. Schelling thus reached the conclusion, earlier than Darwin (from other sources), that humans were products of nature, and that ultimately humans did not come to know nature, but rather that nature came to know itself through humans. It is therefore obvious that natural forms of thought, which developed alongside human development, would describe the world as it is for the given species. Schelling's justification in his philosophy of nature and later also in his philosophy of identity is very persuasive and correlates with the best-known form of Darwinian explanation. This assumes that different animal species have different forms of perception and also, hypothetically, of thought, based on the differences between their cognitive apparatuses, but also due to natural selection, environmental pressures, etc. Only those with the cognitive apparatus that provides the given animal access to the world, so that it is able to best succeed in that world, ultimately survive. In other words: those forms of thinking that did not correspond to the contemporary state of the world were gradually eliminated, and mainly those that enabled and encouraged the survival and reproduction of the species have remained. Of course, Schelling did not consider the disproportionate nature or relativity of these different kinds of knowledge that are delivered through different forms of cognitive apparatuses and, on the basis of Christian theology, he believed in the superiority and highest form of human knowledge. Therefore, he probably did not even deal with the question of the existence of "human" or "inhuman" mathematics, as he only considered the question meaningful from the perspective of the human rational subject. Along with Popper or Darwinists what he aimed for was the conviction that our forms of thought were not different from the natural forms, or even that they could be anti-natural; on the contrary, they were the result of the objectivization of nature, or evolution, as Darwinists would say. Mathematics, as part of these forms of thought, is justified by the fact that, whether we like it or not, it enables humankind to more effectively and be more likely to survive (the calculation of the probability of the occurrence of a phenomena, their nature, laws, etc.); and therefore our brains are capable of such forms of thought.

4.3. Why Do We Perceive Beauty?

How does it work with beauty? Is the perception of something as purposeless and at first sight as useless as beauty even justifiable? While in Mathematics, a general statement on the usefulness and substantiation of calculations appears more or less acceptable, especially when you consider the fact that the process of perception itself is quite computable, is a similar statement for beauty also defensible?

According to several evolutionary psychologists, biologists and other thinkers, the existence of feelings of beauty is not quite evolutionarily unconditioned, but leads to survival, increased effectiveness and the likelihood of survival, or a better quality of life. Such a neo-Darwinian concept of beauty is most acceptable and rationalized for phenomena such as partner selection and sexual attractiveness. The aforementioned research by Glenn Wilson, Devendra Singh, David Perrett et al. documented that the physical attractiveness of a partner could be understood as a process of the perception of evolutionarily significant information relating to age, state of health, hormone levels, cycle phase, genetic predispositions, social status, position, strength, etc. It showed that despite significant personal, cultural, geographic or historical specificities, there were certain universal regularities and laws in the perception of the attractiveness of a partner and in their selection. These were often personalized in the prototype of a young, healthy, "well-built", femininely seductive Venus, or a young, athletic, experienced and thoughtful Adonis. Physical attractiveness frequently serves as a significant indicator of suitable predispositions for the creation of a partnership or the reproduction of one's own genes (Weeden, Sabini 2005). Not only from the perspective of the search for a suitable partner to ensure the survival of one's own genes (a healthy, young, hormonally balanced partner has a greater likelihood of conceiving healthy offspring), but also from the perspective of the quality of genes gained (the likelihood the offspring being attractive and the resultant benefits are greater in parenthood with an attractive partner than with a non-attractive partner). Therefore, Nancy Etcoff believes in the thesis of the survival of the more beautiful (2000).

It has been long believed that "men seem to consciously recognize the importance of physical attractiveness more than women (both straight and lesbian)" (Lippa 2007). The reason for this statement is a conviction that male evolutionary strategy is associated more with the indirect control of the success of their own genetic material and thus also leads to polygamy and more attempts to produce offspring than the female evolutionary strategy (Ridley 1993). The female strategy, as a result of the energy-demanding pregnancy and subsequent education of offspring, suggests a focus on quality including those indicators not visible at first sight (success, intelligence, etc.). "However, experimental research, as well as evidence from online dating and speed dating, shows that physical attractiveness is equally important to men and women" (Fugere 2017). It is therefore generally applicable that if the degree of attractiveness parameter can be considered alongside other comparable parameters, we tend to choose the partners that we like the most (Luo and Zhang 2009; Kurzban and Weeden 2005; Thao et al. 2010).

It is obvious that physical attractiveness is not the only and frequently not even the key factor in partner selection (Eastwick et al. 2011; Eastwick and Finkel 2008; Luo and Zhang 2009; Kurzban and Weeden 2005; Sprecher 1989; Thao et al. 2010), as other personality traits and characteristics may play an equally important, if not an even a more significant role (Apostolou 2011; Apostolou 2015; Buss et al. 2001; Perilloux et al. 2011). These can often be interpreted through game theory and evolutionary psychology.[80] Their unifying factor is an assumption that what we like (whether physically or personally) are the characteristics that promise future pleasure (Démuth 2018a).

In relation to this, Denis Dutton (2010) formulated a general theory on beauty and aesthetic feeling, which presupposes the use of evolutionarily principles such as fashion or art (phenomena and mechanisms which at first sight are very distant from reproduction). Dutton believed that an interest in art was rooted in the ability to express our own qualities in the form of the creation of exceptional, sophisticated, original or artistically well-elaborated objects. He provided the example of the invention of a well-crafted hand axe, which fulfilled both its primary function as a work tool, and a secondary aesthetic function. Its production demonstrated the creator's practical skills, as well as his own specificity, as he crafted the tool exceptionally carefully, precisely and innovatively. It showed off his qualities and gifts. Dutton's aesthetics suggests that the creation of works of art, the beautification of us or our environment, etc. are only protracted instruments of gene competition to assist in their survival in a cultural environment. The creators of works of art demonstrate their qualities, and in the same way as peacocks displaying their tail feathers, they point to certain benefits that might accrue from being involved with them. These do not only have to be practical, such as gaining the most skilful partner, but they can also include the promise of other benefits - they have enough time and energy to spare on such unnecessary and luxurious things as appearance (e.g. beautification does not fulfil a practical function, but it

80 For instance, the attractiveness of an intelligent partner intelligence can be interpreted as a promise of the greater likelihood of the prevention or solution of problems, and the attractiveness of optimism and humour, friendliness and fairness promises easier cohabitation, etc. (Dion et al. 1972; Griffin and Langlois 2006). The same is applicable to the attractiveness of moral qualities such as truthfulness, goodness or faithfulness. The preference for such qualities in a partner occur transculturally (Shaffer et al. 2000; Zebrowitz et al. 2012).

"costs something"), or they can even serve as "evidence of actual interest" and a promise of future consideration for their partner, their cohabitation and offspring in the form of the investment of energy in something that, as such, does not directly fulfil a practical function. Sir David Attenborough convincingly demonstrated that the beautification of the environment, building a nest or gathering engagement objects was not only a matter for the humankind, but was a general natural principle that could be found in various places and in almost all forms of sexually dimorphous animals. The Israeli scientist and biologist, Amotz Zahavi, even formulated a handicap theory, which assumed that a display of beauty (the peacock's tail) and beautification were the expressions of energy demands, which their bearer could afford (unlike others), and thus were a display of the strengths of the bearer. When applied to art: beauty, whether its creation or acquisition, is also an expression of the strengths of its creator or owner.

However, Dutton's approach to the neo-Darwinian interpretation of the origin of art as a means of natural selection and of selection pressure is not always or broadly accepted. There are also theses on the autonomy of art, its transcendental nature, etc. Darwinism itself does not comprehend beauty only as a means of getting a partner or gene preservation. It can be a side effect of other, less evolutionary important processes. Similarly, the development of some areas of Mathematics has not always necessarily been motivated by need to solve practical problems and issues, but sometimes has simply been a consequence of ordinary curiosity, interest or the side effect of searching for answers to other, for instance, aesthetic or architectonic issues.

Despite this fact, this view brings some very interesting and useful interpretations. The perception of beauty by people appears to fulfil a certain important cognitive or emotional function.[81] By perception, we evaluate a great number of perceived objects, but only some of them evoke pleasant aesthetic feelings and a perception of beauty. Based on Husserl's phenomenology, we like something, because it evokes pleasant feelings. Hence, if we see some scenery, an object or a person, or even if we imagine them, our minds evaluate the stimulus - the image, and subsequently the on our body. With "horrible" objects, a quickening of the pulse, a change in breathing, a widening of the pupils, etc., generally what we call fear or alarm typically occurs. With "beautiful objects"[82] the result of their perception

81 Dutton deals with aesthetic instinct (Dutton 2010).

82 To be correct we should probably say objects that evoke beautiful feelings; but, for the sake of simplicity, we say that the objects themselves are beautiful.

is pleasant feelings and their contemplation, i.e. the perception of beauty perception (Drummond 2009, 368–369). Our brain and entire nervous system evaluates the stimuli we encounter, and the result of this evaluation (calculation) is reflected as either pleasant or unpleasant feelings. This occurs when we perceive the sweetness of sugar in our coffee, the heat transferred to thermo-sensitive cells of our skin, as well with works of art. The reasons that some objects are perceived as pleasant or beautiful, while others are not, have been uncovered by evolutionary psychologists, who find justifications or complex algorithms for the construction of aesthetic experience. In the case of the sweetness of sugar, this is due to its huge energy value and its easy utilization by the organism, which gains a large amount of energy without increased exertion.[83] In the case of a beautiful figure, the reason may be its likely reproductive ability, and in the case of abstract art, the reason is its intellectual value, which saturates our cognitive or emotional needs.

To explain the perception of feelings associated with the perception of some internal or external percepts, Antonio Damasio (Damasio 1994) introduced the concept of somatic markers. According to this, organisms evaluate all internal and external impulses at different levels of consciousness. Some processes are a stimulus for a whole range of other mechanisms and processes at an unconscious level, others become conscious by means of, e.g. percepts and emotions. Emotional feelings appear when a decision based on a personal opinion is necessary for the preservation of the organism. These include fear. The perception of an object can evoke an immediate instinctive reaction, which leads to a certain automatic response (such as a reflex), as well as a reaction manifested as a physical reaction and thus an emotional feeling that encourages the organism to certain form of behaviour. In the case of fear, to escape or avoid and in the case of beauty, rather to approach, target and contemplate.

Certainly, some of the contents of our consciousness appear without the need to express a personal opinion. They include mathematical and logical operations and everything that is covered by the term "abstract thinking". Paradoxically, despite the fact that the given contents frequently do not request a personal opinion (on the contrary, any emotional thinking in relation to them is rather more detrimental than beneficial), a personal opinion on the results of such thoughts in the form of emotions (e.g. the view of the beauty of a mathematical proof) can be expressed after all. The

83 Sugar which is relatively easily metabolized, compared to complex metabolization, e.g. that of fat.

fact that we are also able to express an emotional opinion on such abstract mental constructs only proves that our thinking and perception is a holistic process, and that the possible solution to a problem or the form of its solution can affect us (as people) emotionally.[84]

Pleasant feelings, the same as other emotions and feelings, are signals to the organism that the given impulse indicates a different state, e.g. a reward (or a punishment), or a state that is important to the organism. The link between the given somatic state and future rewards or punishments is provided by an evolutionarily or ontogenetically acquired association. The organism thus calculates the possible consequences that result from the evaluated impulses in the form of somatic states and their markers. The experience of beauty is undoubtedly associated with pleasant feelings and with the perception of a value that the organism perceives as desirable, whether with excitement and eagerness, or, vice versa, with tranquillity and durability.

Hence, perceiving beauty can be understood as an evolutionarily and epistemically significant evaluation of impulses and the possible rewards that result from them. Moreover, in the case of aesthetic experience or the perception of beauty, another type of calculation is frequently concerned. It is the comparison of the intensity of the feelings, also including a comparison of the strength of the somatic reaction resulting from the given impulses. Not all impulses are pleasing (these are not promises of an emotional, biological or intellectual reward), and not all of the pleasing ones are perceived as equally likeable. Different levels in the intensity of feelings of pleasure or fancy again suggest that fancy is a result of comparison and calculation.

4.4. Biological Sources of Mathematical and Artistic Beauty

In 2018, Semir Zeki, Oliver Y. Chén and John Paul Romaya published a study uncovering the biological bases of mathematical beauty. According to both classical studies and traditional philosophical interpretation,

84 For instance, because the solution contradicts established opinions and convictions, and we will need to rebuild the whole architecture of knowledge, or, vice versa, that we have solved a problem and removed obstacles, or discovered a way that will bring benefits in the future.

biological and artificial beauties and their sources typically can be distinguished. An aesthetic experience with a biological beauty is characterized by inborn brain schemes, which typically are universal and resistant to change as a result of individual or group experiences. Their effect reaches beyond the original intentions and possibilities of a given individual (people who do not plan to have, or cannot have offspring, seek the same physical characteristics in potential partners). On the other hand, when dealing with artistic beauty, it is mostly considered to have been determined by the schemes adopted soon after birth, and very often under the strong influence of the experience gained by an individual, their education as well as the pressure of the society they live in. "Hence, in terms of aesthetic rating, biological beauty (in which we include the experience of beautiful faces or human bodies) is characterized by less variability between individuals belonging to different ethnic origins and cultural backgrounds or the same individual at different times. Artefactual beauty (in which we include the aesthetic experience of human artefacts such as buildings and cars) is characterized by greater variability between individuals belonging to different ethnic and cultural groupings and by the same individual at different times" (Zeki, Chen, Romaya 2018). A peculiarity of mathematical beauty is "that the experience of mathematical beauty (Zeki et al. 2014), even though it constitutes an extreme example of beauty that is dependent upon (mathematical) culture and learning, belongs to the biological category and obeys one of its characteristics, namely lesser variability in terms of the aesthetic ratings given to mathematical formulae experienced as beautiful" (Zeki, Chen, Romaya 2018).

Zeki et al. assumed that the perception of mathematical beauty was more associated with Chatterjee's concept of cold beauty, which was determined by meaning, contemplation and Damasio's abstract thinking without a need to express one's own position. "The experience of mathematical beauty is derived from a highly intellectual, cognitive source; it is perhaps the most extreme example of aesthetic experience that is dependent upon culture and learning" (Zeki, Chen, Romaya 2018). It could be thus suggested that differences between biological and intellectual beauty would also lead to differences between the neuronal correlates and brain activities associated with the experience of them in our consciousness. Previous research (Zeki et al. 2014, Ishizu, Zeki 2011) had clearly suggested that different parts of the sensory cortex were activated in the perception of visual or musical beauty, and that there was a part of prefrontal cortex (particularly in field A1 of the medial orbital-frontal cortex (mOFC)), which, along with the reward system, recorded increased levels of positive activity in when experiencing beauty or a positive aesthetic experience. With reference to the different nature and complexity of visual and auditory perception from analytical mathematical and abstract thinking, it was assumed that the brain did not react equally to the perception of mathematical beauty, or did it activate the same areas and mechanisms in as different activities such as passive perception and active analytical activity. However, the opposite is true.

As Zeki's research showed, "the experience of mathematical beauty correlates with activity in the same part of the emotional brain as the experience of beauty derived from sensory sources, such as the visual or musical (Ishizu and Zeki 2011)" and moral (Zeki, Chen, Romaya 2018). It led Zeki to the conviction that the essence of mathematical beauty was biological and inborn.

Zeki's argumentation was supported by using a parallel with colour perception. "The colours of objects and surfaces remain constant in spite of wide fluctuations in the wavelength-energy composition of the light reflected off them (Land 1974). This phenomenon is generally referred to as colour constancy although we much prefer the term constant colour categories (see Zeki et al. 2017). Although the colour category does not change with such fluctuations, the exact hue (shade of colour) of a patch belonging to a given colour category may do so. The generation of constant colour categories is due, we suppose, to an inherited brain program, which compares the wavelength-energy composition of light coming from one patch with that coming from surrounding patches, thus generating ratios between the two for every waveband (Land, 1974), with the ratios remaining constant in spite of significant changes in the amount of light of different wavebands reflected from the viewed patch and its surrounds. In fact, psychophysical experiments that have been under taken (in preparation) demonstrate that there is very little variability between humans of different ethnic and cultural backgrounds when asked to assign the colour of patches (when the wavelength-energy composition of the light reflected from them changed) to a standard set of coloured chips. This is due to an inherited brain program for the generation of constant colour categories; the patches do not change their colour categories with such fluctuations. Hence humans can (and do) suppose that others have a similar colour experience to them and that their experience has, therefore, universal, assent[85]" (Zeki, Chen, Romaya 2018).

85 When we speak of similar colour experiences, we restrict ourselves to saying that different humans do not differ when assigning different coloured patches, surfaces or objects to chips that belong to different colour categories. In saying so, we do not address the vexed question of colour qualia.

I am afraid that Zeki's argumentation referring to Kant's and Russell's views of the universality of mathematics and logic, due to the intrinsic structures of thinking and its analogy with colour perception, cannot be accepted. First of all, it is completely obvious that the beauty of mathematical equations or procedures cannot be viewed and subsequently appreciated by everyone, as is the case of the perception of colours. Colours are seen automatically, without the need for extensive personal learning. And although there are some relevant theories that seek to point to interference between our colour perception and intellectual background (knowledge, experience, etc. (Démuth 2009b, Mcpherson 2012)), there is quite a broad consensus on the fact that colour discrimination is fully automatic, without the necessity for a high level of theoretical knowledge. However, this does not apply to mathematical knowledge and formulations. Mathematical truths and relations are not perceived automatically, and we need to be gradually introduced to them. Not everybody is able to perceive or understand the beauty of Euler's formula or Pythagorean theorem. On the contrary, this kind of beauty is expressly associated with education and comprehension (Johnson, Steinerberger 2019; Warren 2019).[86]

The second problem with Zeki's interpretation is the conviction that the unchangeability and universality of mathematical truths and beauty must be associated with biological features, i.e. it is inborn. It is true that numerical operations can be also found in other animal species. "There is evidence that we share the capacity to respond discriminatively to numerosities with a wide variety of species. This has been demonstrated in bees, fish, reptiles, birds, rodents, elephants, monkeys and apes. Electrophysiological recordings from the parietal cortex of monkeys suggest that there are neurons in the lateral intraparietal cortex (LIP) that respond to a greater extent the more objects are presented, and neurons in the fundus of the intraparietal sulcus (IPS) that are coarsely tuned to specific numerosities" (Butterworth, Walsh 2011, 618). And although arithmetic or mathematics comprise of much more than the simple recognition of the amounts of some classes of elements, it appears that our brains actually operate specific structures responsible for mathematical operations; Val-

86 On the contrary, Mo et al. have proved "that humans automatically exhibit a preference for visual and moral beauty without explicit cognitive efforts. Using a binocular rivalry paradigm, they identified enhanced gender-independent perceptual dominance for physically attractive people, and the results suggested a universal preference for visual beauty based on perceivable forms...Findings show that behavioural preferences for beauty are driven by an inherent natural tendency towards beauty in humans rather than an explicit social cognitive processes" (Mo et al. 2016).

entine Sorin Costreie therefore even assumes that "The real world is comprised of mathematical structures, and we adapt to it by cognitively adopting to these structures, so they have been internalized during evolution, and have been assimilated by our mind as innate capacities to perform basic mathematical operations. In fact, our mind mirrors the surrounding environment, and thus the actual world comes to our eyes, mathematically structured" (2012, 143).

Zeki thus argues that "The logical deductive system of the brain, whatever its details, is inherited and therefore is similar in mathematicians that belong other wise to different races and cultures. It is in this sense that mathematical beauty has its roots in a biologically inherited logical-deductive system that is similar for all brains. It is only by adhering to the rules of the brain's logical deductive system that a formulation can gain universal assent and be found beautiful. Any departure from that would mean that it has lost the universal agreement. Implicit in our argument is concept that the experience of mathematical beauty, being the result of the application of the brain's logical-deductive system, is a demonstration that the logical deductive system of mathematical brains, no matter what their cultural background may be, is the same. And since mathematical beauty, in our categorization, belongs in the biological category, it is not surprising that there is significantly less variability among mathematicians in rating mathematical equations as beautiful" (Zeki, Chen, Romaya 2018).

Notwithstanding the Lockean argument that possible universality is not necessarily inborn, but simply a result of acquired structures of language and thinking, the problem of the present argument is the distinction between biological (inborn) and artificial (gained by experience).

The distinction between inborn and gained, or biological and cultural, is rooted in modern philosophy. With the gradual uncovering of the fact that individuals receive their individual specificity from their environment during their intra-uterine development (e.g. auditory stimuli, changes in the levels of hormones and other substances in the bloodstream of the mother, etc.), i.e. before birth, but also with regard to the lack of clarity in distinguishing between the a priori character of dispositions from the perspective of individuals and a posteriori character from the perspective of the species, the distinction between inborn and gained may be ineffective.

In addition, as Josef Šmajs points out (Šmajs 1990), cultural mechanisms cannot be considered as the simple opposite of biological evolution. In the process of evolution, people have developed not only their biological predispositions, such as their form of physical existence, etc. but also their intellectual abilities. Our sensory apparatus is the result of a long-term process of hereditary formation and adaptation of the whole cognitive apparatus to its environment. Therefore, if we have an eye that functions on the basis of the trichromatic "mixing" and evaluation of colours; it is due to the fact that as a species, we have been living long term in an environment with a certain structure of visual stimuli (organisms living underground, e.g. moles, do not have such eyes), and this ability proved to be very beneficial after it developed. Abstract mathematical thinking can similarly be considered as a product of evolutionary development, which is also affected by the determinants of environment, and after this ability had developed in humans, it proved to be beneficial, and therefore, it has not only remained, but it has gradually improved.

The idea of a strict distinction between the biological and the artificial abilities of humans therefore appears to be simplistic and, in certain respects, incorrect. Cultural evolution is a continuation of biological evolution, even though its consequences may frequently act against the original foundations (the destruction of own environmental niche or an entire section of the species by, e.g. war). It is essential to realize that both mathematical thinking and aesthetic feelings are the outcomes of a long-term evolutionary process, whose many parts may be "tightly wired" together due to relative stability of the environment, i.e. they become universal or only slightly resistant to cultural or educational changes, while others develop, especially as a result of the effects of individual experience and social impact.

In this respect, Edmund Rolls presented two basic ways in which the organisms achieved their goals. The first one includes goals defined by genes, such as self-preservation, saturation of fundamental biological needs, hunger, reproduction, etc. The achievement of these goals is typically perceived as pleasant feelings, and can be found in almost all primates possessing an orbitofrontal cortex. The mechanisms of goal achievement can be automatic or associated with (strengthened by) learning. This association is dependent on the previous history of strengthening; the present state of the saturation of needs; the estimated amount of immediately acquired rewards (if rewards are perceived as insufficient or negative, or if they are high, however achievable in distant future, they do not have to lead to strengthening); on the calculated absolute value of the reward or punishment received from the given stimulus after deducting the energy costs of its acquisition (if the effort exerted is inadequate to give the possible benefit, or loss (punishment) prevention, then strengthening does not occur – Rolls 2014, 126). The second is syntactic thinking. Its basis is "a computation with many "if...then" statements, to implement a plan to obtain a reward. In this case, the reward may actually be deferred as a part of the plan, which might involve working first to obtain one reward, and only then to work for a second more highly valued reward, if this was thought overall to be an optimal strategy in terms of resource usage (e. g. time). In this case, syntax is required, because the many symbols (e. g. names of people) that are part of the plan must be correctly linked or bound. Such linking might be of the form: "if A does this, then B is likely to do this, and this will cause C to do this...", The requirement of syntax for this type of planning implies that an output of the language system in humans may allow working for deferred rewards by enabling the use of a one-off, individual, plan appropriate for each situation" (Rolls 2014, 127).

It is obvious that mathematical thinking is part of the latter - syntactic thinking. Its peculiarity is thus not its biological origin, but the fact that despite a certain degree of "independence" from genetically programmed and automatic means of goal achievement, it leads to the same result, achieved by a considerable part of the population independent of their cultural context. This does not happen so often in the evaluation of art, in fact it only occurs rarely. However, both kinds of beauty can be considered to be the ability to calculate and perceive aesthetically exceptional solutions that are completely natural and "grafted on biological grounds".

An essential feature in the perception of beauty is that it is not felt when perceiving something obvious, trivial and unworthy. On the contrary, beauty is an expression of the reflection of something else - something perceived as very valuable. And it does not have to be something absolutely unique and unusual. Exactly the opposite. Beauty can sometimes be seen in ordinary and tiny objects or moments. However, this only happens after we have learned to view the given thing a little atypically, or if we have opened up to its influence upon us, and let it influence us by its beauty - its relatively high complexity and simple organization. Because the substantial question of the perception of beauty is not its metaphysical nature, or how it is created and how it can be described scientifically, but how it influences us and what it actually reveals to us.

4.5. The Metaphysical Meaning of Beauty

Despite the existence of manifold forms of mathematical, natural and artistic beauties, they all appear to have a characteristic in common, the ability to draw our attention to the quality of being of an object - a thing, whether through their exceptional nature, form, method of expression, elaboration, originality, etc., or simply by pointing to their own being. The peculiarity of beauty is that it is not obvious, and in a certain way always surprises and amazes. It is something unusual, something that attracts attention, and encourages us to perceive, contemplate and examine. If an object becomes ordinary and ceases to be surprising, it stops attracting our attention and it loses its attractiveness. On the contrary, beautiful things take our breath away, amaze us and make objects "festive". Their unusual nature is given by their unusual character, their rarity and at the same time that is their value. The perception of the value of beautiful things is their most genuine quality. This is the reason why, when we perceive beautiful objects, situations and notions, we realize that they are beautiful, i.e. valuable, and why, aware of their significance, we seek to perceive their being, to draw the attention of others to it and to share or imitate it. Therefore, we take photographs of beautiful places, we tell others what we liked, we speak and write books about those things that others might be interested in, or we even protect what we are convinced is valuable so that we can preserve for other parts of population, or later generations. We believe that what we see should also be seen by others, especially those we like and care about.

This is also valid for mathematical beauty. As mathematics is frequently understood as the study of the laws of structures, changes and space, what most often amazes us in relation to mathematics is a situation when we encounter something that, at first sight, does not meet our expectations, or if we discover the unexpected, unknown links, relationships and laws. The unusual and unexpected character of some relationships or facts draws our attention and encourages us to make a deeper and more intensive examination,[87] as well as to discover a certain organization of the given elements and their possible comprehension. Thus, beautiful things can always cause considerable surprise and represent a certain intellectual puzzle. A puzzle that suggests, or even calls to be grasped rationally - its organization and to find the relationships that enables us to grasp the given thing, notion, situation or phenomenon.

87 An example of such mathematical interest resulting from "illogicality" was the discovery of the Benford-Newcomb law, suggesting that despite the assumed mathematical probability of the distribution of numbers in many sets of natural data, the leading digit of a number is one (31 %) much more frequently than two (17.6 %), or three (12.5 %). This also applies to prime numbers, Fibonacci numbers, etc.

However, the perception of the beauty of objects is not only an expression of the perception of their unusual and non-trivial forms and qualities. What is special about this perception is the fact that it points to the being of the given object itself. Beautiful objects are perceived as beautiful, while we realize their own being. Their fragility, their possible temporary nature, as well as our need to protect them. This is the reason why beauty often prevents us from destroying things whose beauty we perceive. Barbarians do not perceive beauty; thus it creates no obstacles for them.[88] But if we have to destroy something of the beauty of what we perceive, we have a problem, and a conflict due to the values associated with the existence of the given thing. Therefore, we would rather place it in the world of imagination and mental objects, which are not faded by the destruction of material models and objects. Mathematics has always found refuge in such a world of the immaterial, ideal entities resisting damage or destruction. What is fascinating is the organization and the meaningfulness of being, which are only accessible to reason. The discovery of beauty is thus the discovery of rationality, but also of the value of being of the given forms. And this is greater the better it fits in the context of what we examine.

The perception of the beauty of being of aesthetic or mathematical objects is only a side effect of a deeper aesthetic understanding. The realization of the value or meaning of the being of other things is only possible after (at least an implicit) realization of the significance and value of our own being (Démuth 2019a). Therefore, the beauty of natural, artistic or mathematical objects draws our attention to the value and significance of our own being. If we understand our own existence as not being obvious, and on the basis of the perception of its own significance, we can realize the difference between the ordinary and rare forms of the being of objects and subjects, and appreciate the things in which we find value, compared to those that add less value to our own existence. Beauty thus especially fulfils the value of our being – its perception enriches us, and points to the significance of our own being, frequently not only revealing rare and valuable objects to us, but also by our personal experience of it. Its essence is the perception of a certain pleasure, the identification with own being, fully experiencing it and the perception of its value. With reference to mathematical beauty, this experiencing frequently includes a feeling of participation in something greater, something transcendental in a certain way,

88 We believe that the destruction of cultural monuments or aesthetic objects is only possible if we do not perceive their beauty and significance for our culture, or perceive them to an insufficient extent.

yet something we ourselves participate in due to the revelation of a certain type of organization and complexity, which are the bases for perceiving mathematical, and not only mathematical, beauty. No wonder that the perception of mathematical beauty is often associated with a certain degree of mysticism and transcendentalism.

One of the theses in the book *Beauty, Aesthetic Experience, and Emotional Affective States* is that the purpose of beauty was the search for a better world, and working for it (Démuth 2019a, 146–147). Natural evolutionary mechanisms encourage us to choose those possibilities that should lead to future states considered as suitable or desirable on the basis of the genetic sedimentation of the previous evolutionary experience of the given species or the individual experience of an individual through the perception and preference of beauty. Natural selection and efforts to achieve the best possible outcome thus improve the given species and its environment without us being aware,[89] according to the principles of Bayesian conditional probability. This process results in changes to the initial assumptions, and the continual improvement of the environment with all consequences for the strategies used (i.e. also possible unilaterally applied negative consequences).

The major surprise in this process includes its enormous effectiveness. Animal species have improved as far as possible in order to ensure the highest possible likelihood of their survival with the least possible expenditure of energy. Undoubtedly an advantage of our species compared to others has been the development of an enormously effective instrument for the understanding our own environment, and the possible ways to conquer it in the form of mathematical thinking. Mathematical effectiveness has amazed thinkers throughout its existence. In 1960, the Hungarian-American theoretician and Nobel laureate in (nuclear) physics, Eugen Paul Wigner, gave a famous lecture *The Unreasonable Effectiveness of Mathematics in the Natural Sciences*, in which he reflected on the reasons for the success and preciseness of mathematical research. Wigner viewed mathematics as "the science of skilful operations with concepts and rules invented just for this purpose. The principal emphasis is on the invention of concepts. Mathematics would soon run out of interesting theorems if these had to be formulated in terms of the concepts which already appear in the axioms.... Most more advanced mathematical concepts, such as complex numbers, algebras, linear operators, Borel sets and this list could be continued almost indefinitely, were so devised that they are apt subjects

89 Unless the environment conditions have substantially changed.

on which the mathematician can demonstrate his ingenuity and sense of formal beauty" (Wigner 1960). Despite this, how is it possible that Classical thinkers had already examined elliptic curves long before the discovery of Kepler's laws? How is it possible that the principle of the golden ratio, formulated solely for mathematical purposes by Euclid, clarifies the existence of actual quasicrystals, which were discovered later? And how is it possible that the structure of galaxies with billions of stars can follow the lemniscate of Bernoulli, or that the laws of physics and the world can best be expressed in the language of mathematics? (Livio 2006, 2014).

The present text sought to suggest that mathematics, like sensory perception of beauty, is the result of a long evolutionary journey, through which our species has best adopted to the environmental conditions under which they lived. Our sensory and cognitive apparatus has become sensitive to the stimuli that are important to us in our environment. The same explanation can be used to explain the existence of "an inadequately effective system of abstract thinking" such as mathematics. As Jef Raskin, who started the Macintosh project at Apple, stated, "human logic was imposed on us by the real world, and hence it is in accord with it. Mathematics is derived from logic. Therefore, mathematics is also in accord with the real world" (1998). Its role is basically the same as that offered by perception and related aesthetic emotions - to enable individuals the best probability for survival, as well as the search for a better and more beautiful world. Mathematics does the same. But while in the perception of natural (and partially also artistic) beauty, the pleasure of an aesthetic experience occurs more or less automatically and unconsciously (an analogy of Kahneman's System I - quick thinking), in mathematics, a targeted education and learning using System II - slow analytical thinking - is necessary for the perception of the beauty of abstract and mathematical truths (Kahneman 2011). Obviously, the use of an evolutionarily acquired system for the fast recognition and contemplation of biological beauties may lead to a great degree of uniformity and relatively high level of effectiveness, but also to a certain error rate and mistakes,[90] especially when some essential information from the environment is neglected,[91] or if changes, to which

90 The basis of such an error rate in the perception of, e.g. the attractiveness of a female body may be an inappropriate focus on the Breast-Waist-Hip index as applied to anorexic women, who perceive their waist to be disproportionately large, and therefore reduce their food intake, which, however, results in weight loss from the hips and breast, which then exaggerates the problem.

91 For example, plastic surgery or other modifications of somatic constitution.

we are unable to react, occur in the environment.92 Likewise, the use of an automated system for a quick evaluation of beauty on the basis of personally acquired experience, education, cultural influences, etc. undoubtedly leads to a more or less automatic evaluation of the value of aesthetic objects, although with regard to the diversity of all influences that enter such a process, their level of agreement and binding nature is incomparably lower than that in genetically managed processes. However, their speed and energy demands almost have the character of biologically determined processes. By contrast, mathematical thinking is a relatively slow and demanding process of data evaluation in a certain sequence, determined in advance.[93] Not only do we have to learn it, but frequently we also have to control it. As a result of this, and as a result of the critical nature of mathematical thinking, however, it enables us to eliminate random influences and variables that affect the taste of individuals, which is formed by, e.g. temperament and individual history. This ultimately enables us to achieve incredibly homogeneous results, which are not affected by the subjective determinants of assessment.

The problem with all three types of evaluation of aesthetic stimuli is the different level of their control and learning. While an individual requires no previous experience for the assessment of so-called biological and natural beauties (the algorithms of their evaluation are given by the previous aesthetic experiences of the species), artistic taste is refined by the individual experiences of individuals, and massively influenced by education and the cultural impact of the community they live in. Similarly, mathematical abilities are built on the natural and biological predispositions of the organism; however, their formation is associated with targeted and systematic education and erudition, which not only result in the technical ability to calculate and solve mathematical problems using clearly set procedures and methods, but, at a certain level, also an intellectual insight in problems, enabling us to view broader relations, or even to assess the smartness and beauty of individual approaches and their solutions. Therefore, beauty is not only on the surface of the object that we perceive, but it refers to something deeper, hidden under the surface - to rationality on the surface of an invisible organization. Beauty is in the eye of the one who notices it, in the mind that perceives it and in the brain that first evolutionarily deposited it

92 Relatively quick changes of phenotype on the basis of changes in nutritional accessibility or cultural impacts.

93 It appears that parts of this process can be fully automated through regular practice or even by memorizing (multiplication tables, intuitive solution of ratios or quadratic equations, etc.) Cf. Démuth 2009b.

so it could produce it now. However, it is first of all in the perspective of the interpretation and consideration of things, which is an expression of a specific way to search for a better, formally and rationally arranged being of oneself and the world and its phenomena. This way of perceiving the world (despite its natural character) needs to be learnt,[94] as not everybody is able to perceive beauty as it is presented to them.

94 Evolutionarily developed experience of a species is also learning.

5. Learning to Perceive

We are surrounded by beauties, but we do not recognize them because they come to us so gracefully and seamlessly. We often get inundated with our duties or a common way of thinking, and so we are insensitive to the grace of things and phenomena. The routine or (on the other side) the inexperience often corrupts our ability to see beauty[95] - to see things differently. Seeing the beauty in things, therefore, presupposes some sensitivity, attention, but also the ability to understand things as beautiful. So, to perceive beauty, we need to learn.

5.1. The Beauty of Mathematical Tricks

Children, as well as the children within us, enjoy magic and tricks. Most often they involve an ingenious procedure, which gives the audience the impression that they have entered a magical world, where it is possible to step over the limits of our ordinary world: to walk through a wall, to levitate, take a rabbit out of an empty hat or to read the minds of others.

Mathematics, on its own, seems to be a major trick: together with the results of reflections and experiments in other fields, it has allowed us to build spacecraft, which can take us into space, nuclear bombs with unbelievable destructive power, smartphones, which joins together several previously separate gadgets. If our predecessors from several centuries ago saw this, they would believe it was a kind of magic.

But there are also minor and nice mathematical tricks that are enjoyed by both children and adults, and that are so easy to perform that even children (who can count to around 30) can perform them, all the while hiding their path to the more profound levels of mathematics. Below we will describe one such trick, which could be characterized as mind-reading - it involves guessing the number someone is thinking of based on numbered cards (see Haran 2012).

The trick may look like this: someone from the audience has to think of a number from 1 to 30. He or she may tell it to others or write it down so no one can see it. You have 5 cards with numbers, which are sorted from the lowest to the highest. Ask the spectator who thought of the number to look at all the cards and choose the ones that show his or her number.

95 We lose mindfulness or believe that things cannot be different than we understand them.

Now you only need to glance at the chosen cards (and say a magic spell, if you wish) to be able to tell the astonished spectator the number he or she chose.

This may sound like some sort of wizardry or mind-reading for non-mathematicians, but mathematicians can see beautiful and simple laws in the world of numbers as applied in this trick. Let us examine the easiest way of performing this trick. The first number written on each of the cards is an exponent of the number 2, beginning with the zero exponent, thus 1, 2, 4, 8, 16. Each card then represents a position in the binary numeral system, For instance, the number nine equals 1001 in the binary numeral system, because $9 = 1 \cdot 2^3 + 0 \cdot 2^2 + 0 \cdot 2^1 + 1 \cdot 2^0 = 8 + 0 + 0 + 1$. The number nine will therefore be written on cards beginning with numbers 1 and 8. When the spectator gives you these two cards, all you have to do is add the first numbers on the cards and you will know that he chose the number 9. Each number is attributed a single combination of cards, which means that for each integer written in the decimal numerical system, which we normally use, there is only one way for it to be written in binary, which is used by computers. If we wanted to perform this trick with the numbers from 1 to 100, we would need 7 cards and a bit more practice in mental arithmetic, but the principle would be the same.

This trick not only introduces the binary numeral system and how it is used in computers but is also suitable as an entry point into the more complex world of numerical theories. This has to do with the so-called Brown's criterion (1961). This criterion postulates the conditions for judging if a series of integers is complete; completeness is defined as the ability for each number to be expressed through the addition of the numbers of a certain subset of the given set. To explain this in the language of tricks and guessing numbers, there are also other ways to prepare cards for a trick. We will demonstrate this with two interesting sequences which fulfil Brown's criterion. The first one is the previously mentioned Fibonacci sequence (without the additional number and only for the purposes of the trick, i.e. up to 30): 1, 2, 3, 5, 8, 13, 21 and the second group is prime numbers (with the additional number 1 and again only up to 30): 1, 2, 3, 5, 7, 11, 13, 17, 19, 23, 29. In these sequences there is not more than one way to write the numbers from 1 to 30 as the addition of the numbers in a sequence. And not even all the numbers of the sequence are necessary. With a bit of effort, it would be easy to create cards beginning with different numbers, but the manner of "mind-reading" would be the same: just add the first numbers on the cards with the chosen number written on them. And once again, even a 10-year-old child would be able to perform this trick. Even though the properties of Fibonacci numbers and prime numbers are studied by further mathematics.

There are undoubtedly a lot more similar tricks, which may spark our interest and draw our attention to the degree of organization and the beauty of mathematics. One of the best-known tricks is speed mathematics, which allows relatively large sequences of Fibonacci's numbers to be added very quickly and effectively, since the addition of numbers from the first to the n-th number equals the (n+2)th number minus 1. So, the addition of the first five numbers equals the value of the seventh number (13) minus 1. Similarly, as demonstrated by Carl Friedrich Gauss, it is possible to "add up" the sequence of consecutive natural numbers, for example, from 1 to *k* by pairing them (the smallest with the largest, the second smallest with the second largest, etc.), and then add up these pairs or simply add up the numbers 1 to *k* and divide this (k+1) by two. Obviously, these examples do not involve real addition but rather the use of particular knowledge about the relationships between numbers and their effective presentation. The same applies to knowledge about the relationships between Pythagorean Fibonacci numbers - if the outside members of any group of four consecutive Fibonacci numbers is multiplied, the multiplication of the "inside" members of this group of four numbers multiplied by two and the addition of the squares of the "inside" numbers of this group gives us the three Pythagorean numbers (numbers equalling the lengths of the sides of a right-angle triangle). Furthermore, as proven by Charles Raine, the last number is also always a Fibonacci number (Livio 2006, p. 98). Moreover, Pascal's triangle allows us to identify not only the relationships between the individual numbers (the value of a number equals the addition of the two superposed numbers), but also the value of lengths of the triangle's individual diagonals (the diagonal of ones, the diagonal of natural numbers, the diagonal of triangular numbers, the diagonal of tetrahedral numbers, etc.). Another example of mathematical tricks involves a simple knowledge of the properties of numbers, such as that the addition of the ciphers of any multiple of 9 equals 9, or that when multiplying multi-digit numbers by 11, we have to insert the sum of their ciphers between the first and the last number of the multiplied number. This type of knowledge of mathematics allows us to attract attention to the world of mathematics and focus on things which would otherwise be left unnoticed and thus obscured to us. And this is perhaps the most crucial similarity between beauty and mathematics.

In 2016, V. Rani Satyam from Michigan State University published an article, according to which the important features of mathematical beauty include, in addition to simplicity, conciseness and enlightenment, mainly the moment of surprise. He responded to traditional knowledge, when, for instance, Nathalie Sinclaire specifically characterized mathematical beauty as a visual appeal, connectedness, fruitfulness, apparent simplicity, and indeed, surprise. Similarly, what G. H. Hardy, a famous mathematician, valued the most in the beauty of theorems was their unpredictability. Satyam "through examples, argues that simplicity alone is oftentimes not enough for a piece of mathematics to be considered beautiful, but rather it is unexpected simplicity that we seek. He proposes, moreover, that surprise is necessary for enlightenment" (2016, 196). Oddity, novelty or unexpectedness undermines the obvious and ordinary nature of the perceived object and forces us to pay attention to the closer examination of the new. This causes the observer to focus on what they have not perceived so far as something sufficiently valuable for further meaningful investigation.[96] At the same time, Satyam adds, with the most frequent verbal reactions mathematics students in mind, that "moments of surprise can pique students' interests, whereas constant surprise can turn into confusion and turn students off" (2016, 208). This means that the discovery of an unexpected arrangement and organization or, on the contrary, the discovery of a disruption of the expected symmetries or asymmetries often results in an increase in interest and attention, but only if the surprise and the suspense that arises from it are temporary.[97] If during this unexpected surprise we manage to find a certain form of organization, order, rules and symmetries, we experi-

96 On the example of efficiency and the compressibility of data, Jurgen Schmidhuber explains in his theory the reason why novelty and unexpectedness captures our interest. Beauty is not necessarily interesting. But it is interesting if it is new. A new element and its discovery gives us the chance to not only discover a new piece of knowledge, but also to compress the previously acquired knowledge and make it more efficient. Hence our attention is drawn to it. "In absence of external reward, or when there is no known way to further increase the expected external reward, our controller essentially tries to maximize "true novelty" or "interestingness," the first derivative of subjective beauty or compressibility, the steepness of the learning curve. It will do its best to select action sequences expected to create observations yielding maximal expected future compression progress, given the limitations of both the compressor and the compressor improvement algorithm. Thus it will learn to focus its attention and its actively chosen experiments on things that are currently still incompressible but are expected to become compressible / predictable through additional learning. It will get bored by things that already are compressible. It will also get bored by things that are currently incompressible but will apparently re- main so, given the experience so far, or where the costs of making them compressible exceed those of making other things compressible, etc." (Schmidhuber 2009, 24).

97 "It's important to note that the moment of surprise and juxtaposition he offered was only possible because of the previous, extended experience of equations working-out (leading to solutions). It would be impossible to find aesthetic pleasure in constant change and surprise" (Sinclaire 2008, 34).

ence a feeling of reward, intellectual satisfaction and beauty. But if we fail to eliminate (find regularities in) this unexpected clash with previously formulated or accepted predictions of what we should or should not see, the defence against this long-term intellectual suspense resulting from this situation causes us to refuse to deal with the problem any longer. Discovering anything unexpected may stimulate and motivate us to carry out further investigation, but it leads to confusion and disharmony from a long-term perspective.

The ability to spot unexpected correlations is linked with a more profound problem - the relationship between the implicit preunderstanding and its impact on that what is seen. It seems that what we believe, based on our previous set of beliefs, opinions and convictions, affects what we can or cannot see. Thus, seeing is not a fully automated process - the result of which not only depends on external objective factors, but also on our preunderstanding and the set of all our previous knowledge and experience (Démuth 2013a). With certain convictions in mind, what we see is often limited by what we expect to see. Our perception of a phenomenon is thus often trapped by its possible interpretation. As a result, we do not fully analyse what we perceived and we are only able to identify those aspects, which do not oppose the expected figurative or conceptual frameworks in which we believe. We often tend to simply overlook anything else. The trust we put in our receptors and intellect then on one hand allows us to see and understand what we perceive, but on the other, it often makes us blind to the unexpected elements, phenomena or comprehension. Over fixation on a single possible interpretation or the closeness in principle to anything new makes us blind and numb to surprise or beauty. This equally applies to the ability to explore new theories and discoveries.[98]

The ability to see the unexpected requires a certain degree of openness towards new possibilities and to new perspectives and arrangements. Sometimes we can be quite unaware of this openness, but its essence lies in the small moment of doubt as to whether we saw something correctly and we again focus our attention to the perceived object or phenomenon, hoping that we only looked wrong or counted incorrectly. At other times it can be more systematic. It presumes that there truly are phenomena and situations in the world that, until now, we have been unaware of, and that we see something new. This principle of openness to new things allows us

98 For instance, Columbus's belief that he would find a Western route to India prevented him from seeing that he discovered a New World. For the importance of anomalies and openness to new interpretations, see Kuhn (1996).

to see and identify surprises. It does not tell us specifically what we should see, but only that we might see something new. Perhaps this is the reason why we are ready to look closer and more attentively and be open to new views.[99]

5.2. Are Mathematical Ideas Some of the Most Transformative and Beautiful in History?

Evolutionary perspectives have great potential when reflecting upon the relationship between beauty and mathematics. At their core are observations of the ways in which our brains react relatively autonomously to the aesthetic aspects of the human face, body and others. In addition to this core, there are more recent layers of cultural development. The development of mathematics itself was inspired by beauty, by a fascination in the inner harmony of abstract thoughts and their inner structure. It seems that the milestones in the development of mathematics have counterparts in other areas, ranging from culture to religion. Many of the seemingly highly sophisticated and outwardly more technical advancements, such as the stages of the development of mathematical language and formalism, actually hide from us the tendency to approach reality in prettier and more elegant ways, which can with relative simplicity affect increasingly more complex relations. Another interesting aspect is related to the internal development of an individual, again, ranging from those aspects which happen without our involvement, such as cognitive development, to those where upbringing, education and personal investment, our freedom and overall existential openness play an important role. The lower stages of development, whether they relate to beauty, personal or spiritual growth, have been studied, empirically, relatively well. The higher stages, which have increasingly suggested a relationship between beauty, wisdom, exis-

99 This is often the case in art. If we constantly see only those objects we expect, they start to bore us and do not attract us. Quite the contrary. Oversaturation may lead to kitsch (Démuth 2019a). But if we encounter a completely new way of expressing ideas (such as impressionism, which could create a whole picture expressing the impression of the moment by means of relatively small spots of colour) as opposed to traditional academic art, a new form could attract us and draw our attention. Therefore, a common strategy of many modern artists is merely to shock. Unexpected surprise may spark our attention, which can subsequently analyse and appreciate forms which would otherwise be left unnoticed.

tence and goodness, remain challenges and motivation for the postulation of hypotheses.

Let us first look at the role of mathematics in the wider context of culture. Mordechai Levy-Eichel begins his article *Mathematics as thought* with a provocative question: "Mathematical ideas are some of the most transformative and beautiful in history. So why do they get so little attention?" (2018). He points at the immense difference between how mathematics is seen in the eyes of ordinary people and well-known thinkers on one hand and mathematicians on the other: "For most people, unfortunately, mathematics is a set of confusing, repetitive, formalistic and abstract techniques. Yet this is exactly the opposite of how mathematicians see their own work. Rather, what attracts them, in the words of *The Mathematics Lover's Companion* (2017), by the graph theorist Ed Scheinerman, are "joyful, beautiful" theorems and proofs, which they arrive at through the sweat of intellectual play. Akin to the best poems, they contain truths about the world perfectly expressed".

There might even be more similarities with beauty. If we force a person, who has no interest in music or sense of music, to study musical theory, scales, bars and chords, he or she might consider it dull, formalistic and abstract. However, for a musical composer it is something so obvious that he can freely move in the realm of melodies, making the world richer with his beautiful melodies. Yet, we have to note two differences between them: there are not many genius musical composers or mathematicians but listening to music is way more attractive for most recipients than the understanding of interesting results from the world of mathematics. Furthermore, educational systems normally put much more pressure on children to learn the basics of mathematics than to master abstract musical theory to approximately equal levels. M. Levy-Eichel also realizes this: "In some ways, mathematics is the hardest, and most realistic, art. The German philosopher Martin Heidegger, for instance, offers an example of an influential thinker who misrepresented mathematics as a kind of thinking divorced from the natural world. In the essay *Modern Science, Metaphysics, and Mathematics* (1962), he writes: "In the mathematical project develops an obligation to principles demanded by the mathematical itself". In Heidegger's view, the embrace of mathematics and technology brings a kind of repetitious, routinized, alienating world in its wake. The paradox, however, is that a desire to bypass repetitious exercises is precisely one of the things that motivates mathematicians. Elementary proofs are nothing if not ways to think about something in all applicable cases so that repetitive testing on each possibility is not necessary. Nothing could be more elegant.

Describing technology and mathematical modes of thought as mechanistic and alienating mistakes the result for the process" (Levy-Eichel 2018).

This difference in approaches could probably be applied in a number of other fields as well. Apart from mathematics and piano playing, we could also suggest football, song-writing, diplomacy, company management or any other sufficiently complex activity. For a certain group of people, a specific activity may seem impossible to understand, too demanding for some others to allow them to continue performing it, but for a small group of gifted people it may be a source of fascination, which makes the learning process and the obstacles seem negligible. There is a close link between beauty and pleasure. It seems difficult to find beauty where one is forced to work hard, which at a certain moment starts to be unpleasant, or which might even provoke revulsion. From this perspective, the Heideggerian alienation is not caused by mathematics, science or technology, but rather by our approach to the way we bequeath our cultural legacy to the next generations and its management. It is the task of pedagogical art to inspire others and teach them new things in a way that balances the effort invested with some form of reward. Certain pedagogical systems do not insist that all children master the same knowledge and skill at the same age, but instead approach children differently. Hence, a question arises in the sense of the teaching of mathematics: is it possible to teach it, even at a slower pace, to connect the learning process with the revelation of (not only) its beauties? Of course, the art of pedagogy is the opposite of resignation; it does not focus on what not to teach or to give up when the first sign of an obstacle appears to the part of the child. On the other hand, how accurately can we decide just how much mathematics every person in a modern society needs?

Levy-Eichel looks deeper at the possibilities of mathematics and art and sees them as a subtle stream flowing at the periphery of human culture, which may, however, be formed more intensively, yet less visibly than political power or religion: "Finally, taking mathematical ideas seriously might lead to the discovery that technical ideas are as important as political or religious ones. Taking mathematics seriously might also, counter to stereotypes, lead thinking away from our current preoccupations with culture and power, and back to questions of aesthetics and beauty. Aesthetics and beauty are ever-present concerns in art and mathematics, though seemingly they are minor matters to historians and humanists today, preoccupied as they are with power" (2018).

5.3. Developments in Mathematics, the Transcendence of Previous Levels and Beauty

Let us return back to the generalized form of Levy-Eichel's notion of a paradox, which, it seems, drives the development of human culture! Drill, repetition, routine and alienation is what motivates us to search for ways to do things better, more easily and ultimately in a more beautiful, elegant way, giving rise to a certain pleasant feeling of satisfaction. But in order for these new ways to find their place in culture, a constant pressure for expansion has evolved, which, for some, means new drills and new feelings of alienation. Ladislav Kvasz suggests an interesting and relatively surprising parallel between the development of mathematics and the development of religion.

An important aspect of the development of each of them is the transcendence from one state to another and the shift to a new state, with this process including the aspects of continuity - the preservation of what was, accompanied by an increase in its complexity, thus exceeding what used to be.

When speaking of transcendence, the first connotations which typically emerge are in the context of religion. Kvasz points to the common ground shared by the rationality of mathematics and religion and to the parallels in the development of these two fields (1997). Religion and mathematics exceed the limits of the world of phenomena and experience and refer to something beyond them. Observations of the development of transcendent forms in these areas give us a chance to identify certain parallels. The first highlighted by Kvasz is a major turning point or shift in mathematical thinking, which was the transition from a specific manual for calculations used in Egyptian mathematics to the notion of proofs in Greek mathematics. The Ancient Egyptians were able to solve relatively complex problems (such as the volume of a truncated pyramid) without truly understanding why this particular method worked. They used it just as we use recipes in a cookbook. In contrast, the proof introduced by Euclid in his *Elements* offered reason and an insight into the problem. Manuals or proofs are two distinct forms of mathematical transcendence. Levy-Eichel pointed out the very same difference when commenting on Heidegger's approach to mathematics.

But the situation is not as simple as it seems. Repeatedly proceeding according to a manual usually means performing an unpleasant routine.

Without a proof, it relies on previous experience, on successful feedback after the previous predictions. If such method proves to be successful, it usually means someone had the insight of a genius into the deeper essence of the reality, which allowed him to see something that others had not seen before. This insight may have come in the form of a "revelation", or knowledge which, to say so, arrived on its own, rather than being the result of specific well-thought steps leading to a goal - in this case his work and creations. Such an experience also tends to have an aesthetic dimension, which is usually perceived not only as the experience of the touch of wisdom, presuming the truth, but also with the pleasant experience of being awarded with beauty and harmony. Usually within society, different people contribute to these discoveries to different extents: some are discoverers, others may taste this experience in the process of learning, including its aesthetic side and others are performers, who, perhaps due to time pressures, are condemned to constant repetition and drill.

Proofs moved insight to a higher level. Method already existed, but somehow it was connected to simple knowledge by means of logical rules. Noticing correlations between simple things and their incorporation into a set of logical rules is not obvious. The discovery of a proof, the enjoyable process of learning it, along with the beauty of the insight that takes place and the mechanical memorization of the proof all represent various levels of the contribution of mathematics to abstract beauty. Thus, in relation to beauty, mathematics lives out a paradox: what is beautiful, efficient and effective in mathematics and the place it finds in a culture may bring beauty to some, but bring unpleasant routine to others. If everyone was a great mathematical explorer, mathematics would not have such a high position and reputation as it has today. As if the beauty of mathematics was redeemed by something difficult and painful, just as the greatness and genius of a good doctor is redeemed by the health issues of others.

Another question indirectly related to the main topic is whether repetition and to proceed according to manuals necessarily has to be soulless, forcing people to feel alienated from themselves, or whether it is possible to transcend such attitudes. It seems that a greater degree of automation is essentially associated with a tendency to act soullessly, but history has shown us many ways in which people have tried to comprehend these tendencies and overcome them. Mainly through deliberate practice and by paying attention.

According to Kvasz, the shift from manuals to proofs has a parallel in religion. In religions, the manuals of mathematical calculations correspond to masses - activities with a symbolic meaning, through which people turn to the transcendent. In both cases, a certain activity is performed with no understanding of how it works. In turn, a mathematical proof corresponds to a religious prayer. Both represent a more immediate insight into the course of events. A proof anticipates the logical rules behind seemingly arbitrary thinking and believes in them. On the other hand, a prayer is a belief in the existence of trust and sense within a seemingly chaotic world as well as in transcendence.

While Kvasz identified that the first major turning point in the development of mathematics was related to geodesy and buildings on a practical level as well as to the practical aspects of geometry, the second turning point was represented by the mathematical aspects of the development of cosmological ideas. Specifically, he highlights how Johannes Kepler (1571–1630) and Isaac Newton (1643–1727), who worked at similar periods in history, searched for regularities and harmony in the solar system. Kepler inherited tables that provided data related to the positions of Mars from Tycho de Brahe and was the first person to conclude that its trajectory around the Sun was ellipsoidal. He searched for a simple principle for a specific planet. This approach aimed to assign a characteristic principle to each phenomenon. By postulating the laws of gravity, Newton discovered a more universal law that relates to a number of phenomena on Earth and in the sky. This law does not search for the specific shape of the trajectory but for how it is created, for the forces that operate in the background. According to Kvasz, this turning point corresponds to the religious transition from polytheism to monotheism. In polytheism, different aspects of life are associated with different deities, whereas within monotheism the world is understood to originate from a single source and is subjected to a single and final impact (Kvasz 1997, 119–121).

In his more recent article (Kvasz 2010), Kvasz adds further insights into the driving forces behind the development of mathematics, religion and culture. He defines four approaches to science (especially mathematics and physics), religion and their mutual dialogue. The first level concerns propositions formulated using a language (with which we can agree or disagree), the second concerns the conceptual framework, the third is related to the limits of this framework under the influence of new insights and the fourth concerns the transcendence of a given state of cognition towards novelty, which was not included in the previous level and cannot be derived from it. Kvasz tries to demonstrate that the most important advancements in science do not occur for purely scientific reasons, but that they also unite stimuli and inspirations from other areas. In the text, he highlights the theological motives behind the works of Galileo Galilee,

René Descartes and Isaac Newton: "In particular, we have to realize that Galileo, Descartes and Newton implemented substantial innovations in their work, which radically exceed everything common in their contemporary science. Theological motives play an organic role in the creation of their work: all three of them relied on theological concepts in the sense of the aspects of their system which allow them to transcend their era. Furthermore, we must realize that these aspects are formal. They do not concern what Galileo, Descartes or Newton say about nature but rather the manner in which they say it. Galileo does not employ theological reasoning in any of his specific physical laws, but instead he merely explains that these laws are mathematical in nature. Similarly, Descartes does not support the selection of a specific variable that should be preserved in nature (speed times volume, which he calls the quantity of motion) using theological arguments, but instead he only uses them to justify the invariability of the variable itself. In the case of Newton, it is not the individual laws which are theologically justified, but only the time and space, i.e. the formal framework in which these laws are incorporated. Generally, we can say that these authors use theological reasoning to support the formal aspects of their systems, not the contentual aspects. However, they do not use them to support all the formal aspects of their systems, but only those through which they transcend the previous state of knowledge. The combination of these two characteristics creates the notion of the form of transcendence as the aspect of the physical theories of Galileo, Descartes and Newton which is tightly linked to theological concepts: in the case of Galileo it is the idea of a rational creator, it is Descartes' idea of God's unchangeability and Newton's idea of God's omnipresence" (Kvasz 2010, 228).

The important parallels and mutual impacts of mathematics and religion discussed above could be discussed even further. While Kvasz attempts to unveil, in an almost archaeological way, the deeper layers of our cultural background as the sources of large movements in the development of society, we may as well add further elements to his view. In addition to the search for knowledge and truth which, on top of the impact of the sacred sphere, is mostly represented by religion which points to a desire for perfection, sense and the good, another of the driving motives may be beauty, as a passionate search for the harmony and simplicity of phenomena hidden behind the complex and seemingly chaotic reality. Science, religion and other areas in their highest forms then become the path towards the cultivation and self-cultivation of people, the art of living not only an efficient, secure and enjoyable life, but especially one which is true, good and beautiful.

This dimension of the understanding of philosophy and the role of mathematics in the process of philosophical self-cultivation is discussed by the French philosopher and historian of philosophy Pierre Hadot (2004). Along with other authors such as Xavier Pavie or Martha Nussbaum, he believes that philosophy initially required a more complex effort compared to the way that academic philosophy presents itself today. Nowadays, philosophy focuses way too much on rationality and the cognitive side of people, whereas the original ambition of philosophy was, according to Hadot, the transformation of the philosophizing subject, encompassing areas of experience, emotion, social relationships and a withdrawal from one's own physicality. He comments the role of mathematics in Plato's school: "Geometry and the other mathematical sciences were crucially important in training, but they represented only the first stage in the training of future philosophers. Within Plato's school, they were practiced in a totally disinterested way. Their utility was not considered; instead, since they were intended to purify the mind from sensible representations, their aim was primarily ethical. Geometry was the subject not only of elementary instruction, but also of advanced research; in fact, the Academy was the birthplace of mathematics" (Hadot 2004, 61).

This view of mathematics which considers it to be one of the tools of human refinement and openness towards good and beauty brings us back to the question of how to employ this treasure and how to pass it on to others, so that the ideal concepts promised by mathematics are also true in real life. Below, we will provide two recent examples from the history of mathematics and logic, which prove that it is not really that simple at all.

5.4. Disputes in Mathematics

Discussions and disputes in mathematics reveal that even though mathematics encourages us to enter its mysterious intangible and timeless world, it does not automatically transform people into impersonal and magnanimous individuals. There have only been a few of such clashes over the last 150 years. John D. Barrow in his book about the philosophy of mathematics thoroughly describes some of them, since they substantially distort the deep belief in objective and impersonal discussions. "There seems a surprising amount of room for human preference and intuitive feeling regarding the foundations of the subject. Such a situation, transparently common in many other walks of life, academic or otherwise, is very likely to give rise to disagreements between the participants. In mathematics these quarrels are comparatively rare, but when they do occur they seem to exhibit an extraordinary ferocity and longevity with all manner of unforeseen results. One of the curiosities about the advent of the intuitionist interpretation of mathematics, first in simple form by Kronecker, and then in all-encompassing form by Brouwer, is that both stages were characterized by disputes between advocates of the more conventional formalist" picture of mathematics and the perceived revolutionaries who sought to impose a new definition of mathematics upon everybody else. The first of these battles was between Kronecker and Georg Cantor, the other between Hilbert and Brouwer, although others were peripherally involved in both cases. These clashes reveal interesting things about the participants and their beliefs and, at the time, played an important role in accelerating the development of the constructivist philosophy of mathematics" (Barrow 1992, 198–199). These disputes had a detrimental effect on the personal lives and relationships of the parties to the disputes and what is more, they were transmitted to the universities, state institutions and also affected the publication of the most prestigious mathematical journal (Barrow 1992, 192–226).

Hence, even mathematics involves certain important concepts which are intuitively understood by some but not by others. The question of what part beauty plays in the process will probably remain unanswered for a long time. One such concept is that of infinity. The peculiarity of the term "infinity" has already been suggested through Zenon's paradoxes. On one hand, Zenon reasons that is it impossible to infinitely divide space and time, but the opposite assumption that space and time are finitely divisible heats up the debate. The discovery of paradoxes in the theory of sets at the turn of the 19th and 20th centuries was considered a disagreement over the fundamental principles of mathematics and science. Again, the key subjects were infinity and self-reference. This led to the postulation of three programmes to overcome this crisis: logicism, intuitionism and formalism. The representatives of these movements argued over the concepts for the basis of mathematics. Not only through calm, peaceful discussions, but also through heated debate, including those mentioned above. If it is difficult to reach an agreement, even in mathematics, which is a sort of showcase for rationality, then it starts to resemble the situation in aesthetics. Perhaps mathematics and aesthetics do not differ significantly over the possibility to reach agreement, but only in its degree, particularly when the aspects of beauty are the subjects of discussions.

5.5. Fascinated by Ideas

The fragility of mathematical beauty is revealed not only through serious disputes, but also by phenomena which look like the opposite: scientific or commercial success, awards and cultural influence that may result in an immense amount of fascination, which can be hard to resist. One of the works which managed to do this and that is not only filled with mathematics but also with art, is the phenomenal work of Douglas Hofstadter entitled *Gödel, Escher, Bach: An Eternal Golden Braid*, or shortly GEB (1979). Shortly after it was published, the book was awarded with two major prizes: the Pulitzer Prize and the National Book Award. It also enjoys academic interest; Massachusetts Institute of Technology provides courses based on it (parts of it are available on YouTube), but it is also possible to attend such courses, for example, in Brno as well. The book is remarkably complex: it addresses the topic of mathematics and beauty, but it also touches upon the brain and mind, the musical form of fugue, syntax, semantics, Zen Buddhism, free will and many others. It is also comprised of several interlinking and self-referential levels. It includes a large number of figures and schemes and explains the connections between seemingly distant fields. Thanks to this complexity it has sparked the interest of many people, yet the author complained, in the new foreword to the book on the occasion of its jubilee publication in 1999, that few people understand what the book is really about: "Many people think the title tells it all: a book about a mathematician, an artist, and a musician But the most casual look will show that these three individuals per se, august though they undeniably are, play but tiny roles in the book's content. There's no way the book is about those three people! Well, then, how about describing GEB as "a book that shows how math, art, and music are really all the same thing at their core"? Again, this is a million miles off - and yet I've heard it over and over again, not only from non-readers but also from readers, even very ardent readers, of the book. And in bookstores, I have run across GEB gracing the shelves of many diverse sections, including not only math, general science, philosophy, and cognitive science (which are all fine), but also religion, the occult, and God knows what else. Why is it so hard to figure out what this book is about?" (Hofstadter 1999, P-1).

For this reason, he decided to dedicate the entirety of the new foreword to the interpretation of the main theme and main lines of thought, a "statement of my religion" (Hofstadter 1999, P-23). Eventually even this did not seem sufficient and as an interpretation of the original book GEB, he wrote another book entitled *I Am a Strange Loop* (Hofstadter 2007). He admits that the main concepts in the book have matured and fascinated him from his teenage years. He describes it concisely as follows: "In a word, GEB is a very personal attempt to say how it is that animate beings can come out of inanimate matter. What is a self, and how can a self come out of stuff that is as selfless as a stone or a puddle? What is an "I"...?" (Hofstadter 1999, P-2) or "the parallel between Gödel's miraculous manufacture of self-reference out of a substrate of meaningless symbols and the miraculous appearance of selves and souls in substrates consisting of inanimate matter" (Hofstadter 2007, xiii).

Of the numerous analyses of Hofstadter's main ideas of how the human self and consciousness is born, we particularly enjoyed the article by Adam Westra (2010). He attempts to untangle the web of Hofstadter's analogies, metaphors and examples of various aspects of culture, the core of his approach to the issue. Hoftsadter himself made the untangling easier by including the phrase "strange loop" in the title of the second book. Referring to quotes from the book *I Am a Strange Loop* (abbreviated to SL) Westra interpreted the core as follows: "This is where the central analogy with Gödel's "Incompleteness Theorem" comes in: according to Hofstadter, Gödel's great discovery consisted in showing, by means of a sophisticated mapping technique, that the formal system contained in Russell and Whitehead's Principia Mathematica inevitably produces, because of its universal representational capacity, certain self-referential statements, or "strange loops". An analogous phenomenon is just as inevitably produced in the brain, and this, combined with humans' "innate blindness" to the inner workings of our own brains, i.e. "our inability to see, feel or sense in any way the constant, frenetic churning and roiling of micro-stuff, all the unfelt bubbling and boiling that underlies our thinking" (SL, 204) effectively makes us hallucinate an "I", a Self which - or rather, who - seems to run the show, i.e. whose apparent causal agency according to beliefs and desires feels like the "realest" thing in the world (SL, 202). In a word, the "I" is not the starting-point, but rather the gradual outcome of a complex process of perception that twists back on itself, thereby giving rise, over time, to an ineradicable, yet indispensable, illusion: "I" (SL, 204). Again, Hofstadter is not necessarily trying to prove this claim as a definitive theory of consciousness, but rather sees himself as offering a new perspective on the mind, a sort of "Copernican Revolution": "My claim that an "I" is a hallucination perceived by a hallucination is somewhat like the heliocentric viewpoint - it can yield new insights but it's very counterintuitive, and it's hardly conducive to easy communication with other human beings, who all believe in their "I's with indomitable fervor" (SL, 293). More fundamentally, Hofstadter offers a distinctive vision of the human condition (or at least a new variation on an ancient and recurring theme): insofar as we cannot help believing in the "story" we tell ourselves - namely, that each one of has, or rather is, an "I" - it then follows that "the human condition is, by its very nature, one of believing in a myth" (SL, 295)" (Westra 2010).

Equally he comments on the problematic point of Hofstadter's analogy between the proof of Gödel's Incompleteness Theorem and the formation of consciousness. Hofstadter's analogy for the evidence of Gödel's theorem was as if they suggested that strange loops are formed in any sufficiently massive formal system both automatically and necessarily. On the other hand, when interpreting the evidence, he states that the way Gödel created the strange loops is complicated, artificial and thorough, which implies that there is nothing natural or necessary in it. This argument denies the analogous spontaneity and necessity for the creation of consciousness from the smallest physical entities of the universe, beginning with quarks and neurons. However, if Gödel's strange loops are the result of conscious thought, what does consciousness result from? Westra also explains the difference between the necessary and sufficient condition in logic: "... the representational power of the formal system described in *Principia Mathematica* is merely the condition of the possibility of the emergence of a strange loop, not its cause (in logical terms: a merely necessary, not a sufficient condition)" (2010).

Hofstadter expects to have opponents and offers answers to a number of diverse objections. Westra's analysis can be understood as a spotlight shedding light onto the profound layers of Hofstadter's thinking, which is seemingly fascinated by Gödel's discovery of the creation of meaningful assertions from a sufficiently rich system of graphemes without any meaning. However, what fascinates Hofstadter and the direction of his intuition is not familiar to others, as their intuition offers them the exact opposite of what is offered to Westra: it is not the strange loops which created consciousness, it is (Gödel's) consciousness that created strange loops.

Several similar opposing intuitions can be found in history. In relation to possibility and realization, Aristotle ontologically preferred realization, the actuality. But the approach of this materialistic evolutionist is the exact opposite: it prefers potential. It is not a coincidence that Hofstadter mentions Zen Buddhism; his understanding of the self as a myth resembles the Buddhist term *anatman* (the opposition of the self, *atman*). These are examples of another pair of opposing intuitions that originated in India, both of which attract supporters and followers: the Hinduist *atman* and Buddhist *anatman*. This is similar to the situation where mathematicians throughout history have tried to decide whether the notion of infinity is intuitively well-understood or not. As we have demonstrated above, their views differed.

It seems that the preference for certain explanations of the nature of reality in the depth of our myriad convictions is, after all, determined by our intuition, which decides what is closer to us, what appears to be more harmonic or beautiful; it represents a strange sort of type of aestheticism in the core of decision-making for basic possibilities. However, it is perhaps a different type of beauty than the one we experience day to day through the beauty of a face, picture or landscape. Even some of the above-mentioned examples show that it is not merely a rational aspect of our view of the world; it includes passions, determination, fascination, all of which relate to beauty. As we are writing this, we do realize that at our deepest level of decision-making we are governed by the aestheticism of our own intuition. We are fascinated by Hofstadter's majestic work and although we do not agree with his basic intuitions about the nature of self and consciousness, it might be the oddity of his views, the mirror that he provides that helps us better assume the roots of our own convictions.

The fragility of mathematical beauty that we have highlighted does not harm it; quite the contrary, it makes mathematics valuable. Just as Gödel and his proof suggested that the development of mathematics and new knowledge cannot be completely formalized and programmed processes, they will always primarily be a creative human activity, the cultivation of people, spirituality and the contribution of mathematics and beauty to the process will remain art rather than an algorithmic process.

6. Conclusions

In this book we have attempted to outline the view of a philosopher - a cognitive scientist, a psychologist and a mathematician - theologian on the topic of the relationship between beauty and mathematics, their importance and what they reveal to us. The authors of the book are aware of the fact that beauty is primarily linked to subjective feelings, individual - personal experiences, feelings of liking, enjoyment and charm, as well as with perfection and aesthetic or existential fulfilment. We know that even the finest nuances of aesthetic experiences are very subjective, often personal and individual, and hard to express through language. On the other hand, equally we see that despite the aforementioned subjectivity, beauty exceeds us, that despite its personal experience it is something we want to share with others, it is something we tend to objectivize. We discuss beauty and what accompanies its perception as something that is independent of us, something with its own logic, regularities and rules. We strive to comprehend it, often in a very inaccurate and perplexing way, but hoping that what we feel and experience is sufficiently accurately comprehensible and capable of being expressed in a language - in particular by means of a mathematical language. For, since time immemorial, mathematics has been characterized by an accuracy and preciseness of expression, as a reference to the objective, using mathematical formulae and objects that are describable in that relation. It is no coincidence that the first culturally most significant thematization of beauty is linked to the Egyptians, the Babylonian, but mainly to Pythagorean mathematics and theology. It was the Pythagoreans and their predecessors who discovered explanatory and methodologically very important tools to describe beauty and its characteristics. These tools were numbers, which allowed them to describe the relationships between diverse entities, regardless of their contents and focusing only on their number, order or a comparison of their qualities. Numbers thus became a language that enabled the expression of crucial characteristics of virtually anything in a very precise and objective manner. It is no wonder that they became a divine and universal tool for the Pythagoreans - not only did they successfully express all content and form using numbers ("Everything is a number"), but they also reflected the real characteristics and principles of the universe, hidden in all of the world's phenomena as kinds of "divine archetypes" (protoprinciples) which are revealed to people through a thorough study of the universe. The power of mathematics and numbers are linked to two aspects of beauty. The first is that despite the fact that the aesthetic experience and the experience of the perception of beauty can be immensely diverse in its content and yet subjective, one of the best tools to understand it and objectively describe it is numbers. The intensity of subjectively experienced beauty can be measured by numbers (on a scale from 1 to 10), just as can be the frequency of its occurrence. We may equally objectively describe or express the degree of any attribute using, for instance, grammatical (mild/pretty, strong/prettier, the strongest/the prettiest) or any other type of gradation. The mutual comparison of evaluations and preferences allows us to make objective ratings and rankings, expressing general preferences for elements or phenomena in the studied populations (by means of observations, questionnaires, scales, tests, experiments, etc.), to explore or quantitatively define seemingly exclusively qualitative indicators. Mathematization and the processing of statistical data subsequently allow us to define the individual relationships, correlations and distributions of phenomena as well as to create models to predict the probability of their occurrence or the randomness of phenomena, the degree of significance, validity and reliability of the research. Since the era of Pythagoras and Euclid, arithmetic and geometry have allowed us to study and visualize a number of phenomena, relations and patterns and to objectively describe what characterizes them. The duration of our gaze, when observing beautiful objects, the reaction time necessary to record and evaluate them, the accuracy of the evaluation as well as the intensity of the experience can be expressed by quantifiable indicators. It is equally possible to geometrically describe the trajectory of our gaze, aimed towards what we like, the progression of physiological changes that accompany an aesthetic experience (an increase in galvanic skin response, blood pressure, accelerated heart beat and breathing, pupil dilation, change of muscle tone, etc.), but also the different activity and distribution of, for instance, the individual brain centres during the assessment, evaluation or feelings from an aesthetic experience. What is more, not only are these activities and phenomena based on different forms of computational processes, but their imaging requires highly complex and sophisticated forms of calculation, allowing the comparison of various activities, processes, evaluations and saturations; and their imaging consists of these computational and imaging mechanisms and processes. Due to the use of these mechanisms and the conceptual inventory of game theory or the calculation of the extent of rewards based on the amount and the structure of the energy used, complex phenomena such as biological, evolutionary, neuroaesthetics, as well as psychological, anthropological, socio-economic or neuro-marketing and neuro-ethical and various other aspects linked to the brain reactions to certain aesthetic impulses (e.g. beauty of the face, of the human body, etc.) can be adequately explained, in a scientific and mathematically understandable manner.

On the other hand, the relationship of mathematics and beauty is not only represented by the language and the tools which can be used to describe it. As assumed by Pythagoras and Plato, many philosophers believe that mathematical laws come from the essence of beauty and its structure. The search for beauty and its objective description draws our attention to the organization of its manifestations, to the complexity and harmony between the parts and the whole, to their perfect well-fitting relationships. Finding these logical, rational and well-fitting relationships convinces philosophers that not only is beauty capable of being described by mathematics, but that it is itself of a mathematical nature.[100] Harmonies, symmetries, proportions and resemblances found in the world encourage thinkers to believe that nature, the world and space are organized by logical and mathematical laws and relations. Hence even completely abstract concepts such as mathematical formula that expresses these laws can be seen as beautiful, because beauty not only lies in the form in which these relationships are expressed,[101] but primarily in the fact that the world itself is governed by these "beautiful proportions".

---

100 Yet, as John L. Bell shows, there is a fundamental difference between art and mathematics: "Mathematicians are moved - almost to the point of tears - to behold the timeless realm of mathematics, in which beauty is so closely allied to truth. Indeed, the first half of Keats' dictum, *Beauty is truth, truth beauty* is held by mathematicians to be realized in the mathematical realm. Not, however, the second half, since there are plenty of mathematical assertions which, while undeniably true, can hardly be described as beautiful. This fact points up one essential difference between the world of mathematics and the world of art or music - close as they are in many respects. The artist or musician has a high degree of control over the world he or she creates through the production of art or musical works. The artist can choose to create works of art that are surpassingly beautiful, or shockingly ugly (especially in contemporary art!) The mathematician has no such freedom (except in the production of expository works) for in the end he or she is constrained by the dictates of mathematical truth and proof. Here we recall Eddington's observation: *Proof is the idol before whom the pure mathematician tortures himself.* The artist can actually *set out* to produce a beautiful painting, or the composer a beautiful piece of music (according to their lights, at least). The mathematician, subject as he or she is to the imperatives of the two idols, truth and proof, tends to be surprised when something of genuine beauty emerges from his endeavours. Again, Brouwer would probably have dissented from this view, since he saw mathematics rather in the way that artists see art, namely as a free creative activity grounded in - or at least guided by - intuition, rather than a struggle to attain some absolute standard of truth" (2015).

101 "Plato was so steeped in Pythagoreanism that he structured his dialogues by counting numbers of lines and placing important passages at points in the dialogue that correspond to important ratios in Pythagorean harmonic theory (Kennedy, 2010 and 2011). Thus, the vision of the form of beauty appears 3/4 of the way through the *Symposium* by line count and the ratio 3 : 4 corresponds to the central musical interval of the fourth" (Huffman 2016).

Hence, the Pythagoreans gave divine meanings not only to numbers, but also to the harmony of the celestial spheres, individual ratios and relationships and believed that the world was perfectly and harmoniously organized. Similarly, Plotinus[102] and Lord Shaftesbury believed that beauty lies in the symbiosis of the parts with the whole, in the proportionality, which exists independently and that the role of man is to unveil it and observe it. The idealist aim of philosophy was thus a search for harmony and proportionality in the world, which is only possible if we understand the true relationships and proportions between things and their parts. Thus, according to Shaftesbury, it is necessary to step back from the details and see the bigger picture. Mathematics lets many thinkers see the bigger picture and forces them to contemplate the essence of the order, what organizes it and where it comes from.[103] For this reason, many of them think beyond the limits of common sense and aim higher with their thoughts - towards the highest objectives of thought. For example, Shaftesbury's concept presumed the possibility of observing the relationships between the different parts of the world from the position and perspective of the eye of god - from the perspective of the creator - in order to see the fitness of the whole and its individual components.[104] Thus, beauty is for many con-

102 "Only a compound can be beautiful, never anything devoid of parts; and only a whole; the several parts will have beauty, not in themselves, but only as working together to give a comely total. Yet beauty in an aggregate demands beauty in details; it cannot be constructed out of ugliness; its law must run throughout" (Plotinus, 21 [Ennead 1.6] in Sartwell 2017).

103 After all, the laws of mathematics are true everywhere (omnipresent), eternal (true always), cannot be defied or defeated (omnipotent) and they are rational and have language characteristics (which makes them personal). Omnipresent, omnipotent, eternal, personal... like God. No wonder mathematics often leads to a certain form of mysticism and religion.

104 As Volker Kessler puts it, paraphrasing Bohren's work *God's Becoming Beautiful* (*Dass Gott schön werde*), "Mathematicians disagree about whether mathematical theories are created or discovered. The majority of mathematicians regard mathematical reality as something outside of us. If we share this view, we could argue: Every time a mathematician discovers a beautiful formula, they discover something that God created. Thus, the mathematician contributes to the visibility of God's beauty in his creation. This would correspond with Bohren's viewpoint that God becomes beautiful in the creation (Bohren 1975:94–99). If, however, we follow the minority's viewpoint, namely that mathematics is a creation, then it would correspond with Bohren's chapter 'Culture and arts'. In that chapter, Bohren (1975:100) argues that God becomes beautiful by and through human creations in culture and arts. Thus, in both cases, we can conclude: *God becomes beautiful in mathematics*. This conclusion may be reached, whether a mathematician believes in God or not. Bohren (1975:105) stresses that God also becomes beautiful through those who do not know Him. For example, Russell and Hardy, two mathematicians often quoted in this essay, were self-confessed atheists. Nevertheless, Bohren would argue that God became beautiful in their mathematical work. Even the French reformer John Calvin (1509–1564), who used to distinguish clearly between Christians and non-Christians, taught that the Spirit of God might

nected with Unity, Truth and Good and touches on the supreme values of existence. This is connected with the more remarkable moment of the aestheticizing of mathematics and mysticism.

While mathematics, at its relatively most fundamental levels of analysis, offers us the tools to achieve the most accurate and precise description of the individual elements or phenomena, the ongoing discoveries of new perspectives on the issue of beauty reveal to us the incompleteness and the fundamental aspectuality of the previous views. What is more, we are gradually discovering the overall incompleteness of the mathematical description of the world (Gödel) and the necessity to change or update individual perspectives. This fact ultimately compensates for any exaggerated optimism which could possibly result from the initial research that asserts that beauty can, to an extent, be mathematically analysed. Although the initial mathematical knowledge of certain types of beauty can be described using algorithms and has the greatest potential to become generally accepted, owing to its accuracy and ability to be verified, ironically, it says the least about the essence of beauty as a whole, despite its exactness. On the contrary, the more complex approaches (incorporating views from several possible perspectives) can say much more about the essence of aesthetic experience, but, unfortunately, at the cost of a certain loss of accuracy and detail of view, which leads to a certain degree of openness and metaphor in the nature of thinking. Ultimately, the maturation which comes hand in hand with the process of discovering and changing perspectives resembles the above-mentioned Japanese aesthetic ideal of wabi sabi, which presumes that completeness and perfection are not only elusive, but also undesirable in a certain way. Their elusiveness lies in the methodological inability to combine the width of the perspective with its sharpness and absolute precision. Either we are able to focus our attention on more accurate descriptions or we can try to understand it as holistically as possible. As Heisenberg's uncertainty principle teaches us, it is not quite possible to precisely describe both at the same time. Quite the opposite. The gradual discovery of new knowledge and laws through changes in individual perspective presents a call for progress and improvement. This may be the reason why a higher degree of understanding is associated with an awareness of its limits and incompleteness, as well as the desire for its fullest attainment (Cusanus). This is only possible through the discovery of new perspectives and their association with the knowledge that has already been acquired.

---

even work through ungodly mathematicians...Therefore, I trust that there is now enough evidence for my initial statement: *God becomes beautiful in mathematics...*" (Kessler 2018).

The exploration of different perspectives provides a further benefit. In addition to extending and generally linking our own knowledge and the phenomena that constitute it (see Hofstadter's theory of "I" - Hofstadter 2007), thus enabling a better understanding of ourselves, a change of perspective allows a better understanding of others and our connections to them. Changing perspectives is a basic pillar of the ability to empathize and sympathize, or the ability to look at an issue from the perspective of the other person. And as we know (e.g. Démuth 2019a), empathy as the ability to understand the contents from the position of the other person is a precondition of the possibility to sympathize and thus to eliminate our own self-centredness in favour of pro-social behaviour and the common good. The English clinical psychologist Simon Baron-Cohen is even convinced that it is the ability to empathize, which makes us moral beings and that a lack of empathy and the inability or unwillingness to perceive problems from another perspective is the fundamental reason and source for the existence of the evil (2011).[105] But whether it is one way or the other, it seems that the perception of beauty, as with the mathematics we keep discovering within it or, on the other hand, the beauty of mathematics, forces us to exceed ourselves - to transcend - whether to something higher outside of us or towards other possible perspectives. And this is where beauty and mathematics lift the spirit and motivate us to become better, higher-quality and perfect people. The way in which they do it,[106] but also their impacts are often quite similar, although their degree of difficulty may greatly differ.[107] In spite of this, their development brings people closer to tolerance

105 In contrast, the psychologist Paul Bloom argues that empathy and sympathy limit rationality and bring inequalities among people, and thus it is empathy, which may be considered the source of evil (Bloom 2016).

106 Natural, spontaneous and sensory-intuitive path of beauty vs. intellectual and rational path of mathematical education.

107 As stated by John L. Bell: "I believe that the unpopularity of mathematics stems largely from the fact that the beauty of mathematics resides almost exclusively in the realm of the intelligible: it is thus regarded as «dry» and «difficult». In this regard music, which abounds in sensible beauty, offers a striking contrast. Musical activity involves three overlapping but essentially distinct classes of people: composers, performers and listeners. Composers and performers respond to both the intelligible and sensible beauties of music, while the vast majority of listeners respond solely to its sensible beauties. In (serious) mathematics, on the other hand, these three categories are collapsed into one. Yet mathematics is not intrinsically more difficult than music. at least in terms of the acquisition of technique. Mathematicians and musicians alike strive to develop and perfect their techniques. The difference is that the (performing) musician's struggle to perfect her art is finally crowned with popular success: no matter how difficult it may be to play a Beethoven sonata, a Paganini caprice, or to lay down an intricate jazz improvisation, an untutored ear can enjoy listening to, and respond to the beauty of the piece, despite lacking the slightest idea of how to play it. By

and perfection - exactly in the spirit of Beethoven's credo: "Do not merely practice your art, but force your way into its secrets; it deserves that, for only art and science can exalt man to divinity" (1892, 627).

contrast, the beauty of most mathematical creations is appreciated only by those mathematicians who are able, like performers of music, to recreate the mathematical work. Mathematics would, I believe, become more popular if, in teaching the subject at the elementary level, greater efforts were made to convey its beauty - albeit of a purely intelligible kind - to students. To set the ball rolling, one might present examples of beautiful mathematical theorems whose meaning is readily grasped. These could include the Pythagorean Theorem, the theorem that there are exactly five regular polyhedra, Euler's polyhedron formula $V - E + F = 2$, Lagrange's theorem that every number is the sum of 4 squares, and the 4-colour theorem. Everyone is capable of appreciating the beauty of truths like these. All could then join Keats in drinking Newton's health, without further wishing, as did the poet, «confusion to mathematics»" (2015, 179).

7. References

Aharon, I., Etcoff, N. L., Ariely, D., Chabris, C. F., O'Connor, E., Breiter, H. C. (2001): Beautiful faces have variable reward value: fMRI and behavioral evidence. *Neuron*, 32, 537–551.

Akiba, F. (2013a): Natural Computing and Computational Aesthetics. Y. Suzuki, T. Nakagaki (eds.): *WSH 2011 and IWNC 2012*, PICT 6, 117–118, Tokyo: Springer.

Akiba, F. (2013b): The Significance of Natural Computing for Considering Computational Aesthetics of Nature. Y. Suzuki, T. Nakagaki (eds.): *WSH 2011 and IWNC 2012*, PICT 6, 119–129, Tokyo: Springer.

Alley, T. R., Cunningham M. R. (1991): Averaged faces are attractive, but very attractive faces are not average. *Psychological Science* 2 (2), 123–125.

Antonsen, R. (2015): *Metaphors, Mathematics, and the Imagination*. TEDx Oslo. [Online] Retrieved [2018-10-20] from: <https://www.youtube.com/watch?v=lv9QDjw8GJk>.

Apostolou, M. (2011): Parent-offspring conflict over mating: Testing the tradeoffs hypothesis. *Evolutionary Psychology* 9, 470–495.

Apostolou, M. (2015): Parent-offspring conflict over mating: Domains of agreement and disagreement. *Evolutionary Psychology* 13 (3), 1–12.

Aristoteles (1996): *O duši*. Praha: Petr Rezek.

Aristotle, [Barnes, J., (ed.)] (1984): *The Complete Works of Aristotle, The Revised Oxford Translation*. Volumes I and II, Princeton: Princeton University Press, 1984.

Atalay, B. (2006): *Math and the Mona Lisa: The Art & Science of Leonardo da Vinci*. New York: Harper Collins Publishers.

Baron-Cohen, S. (2011): *Zero Degrees of Empathy: A New Theory of Human Cruelty*. London: Penguin/Allen Lane.

Barrow, J. D. (1992): *Pi in the Sky: Counting, Thinking, and Being*. New York: Oxford University Press, Back Bay Books.

Barrow, J. D. (2002): *The Book of Nothing: Vacuums, Voids, and the Latest Ideas about the Origins of the Universe*. New York: Vintage.

Beethoven, L. v. (1892): Letter to Emilie, July 17, 1812. *Musical news*, 3, 627.

Bell, C. (1914): *Art*. London: Chatto & Windus.

Bell, J. L. (2015): Reflections on Mathematics and Aesthetics. *Aisthesis. Pratiche, linguaggi e saperi dell'estetico*, [S.l.], 8 (1), 159–179, [Online] Retrieved [2018-12-11] from: <http://www.fupress.net/index.php/aisthesis/article/view/16215/15171>.

Berkeley, G. (2003): *A Treatise Concerning the Principles of Human Knowledge*. Mineola: Dover Publication.

Birkhoff, G. D. (1933): *Aesthetic Measure*. Cambridge, MA: Harvard University Press.

Blood A. J., Zatorre, R. J., Bermudez, P., Evans, A. C. (1999): Emotional responses to pleasant and unpleasant music correlate with activity in paralimbic brain regions. *Nature Neuroscience* 2, 382–387.

Bloom, P. (2016): *Against Empathy: The Case for Rational Compassion*. New York: Ecco.

Borkenau, P., Brecke, S., Möttig, C., Paelecke, M. (2009): Extraversion is accurately perceived after a 50-ms exposure to a face. *Journal of Research in Personality* 43 (4), 703–706.

Brown, J. L. (1961): Notes on complete sequences of integers. *The American Mathematical Monthly* 68 (6), 557–560.

Buss, D., Shackelford, T. (2008): Attractive women want it all: Good genes, economic investment, parenting proclivities, and emotional commitment. *Evolutionary Psychology.* www.epjournal.net - 6 (1), 134–146.

Buss, D., Shackelford, T., Kirkpatrick, L., Larsen, R. (2001): A half century of mate preferences: The cultural evolution of values. *Journal of Marriage and the Family* 63 (2), 491–503.

Butterworth, B., Waslh, V. (2011): Neural basis of mathematical cognition. *Current Biology.* 21, 16, 23/08/2011, R618–R621.

Cao, H. H., Han, B., Hirshleifer, D., Zhang, H. H. (2011): Fear of the unknown: Familiarity and economic decisions. *Review of Finance* 15 (1), 173–206.

Carleton, N. R. (2016): Fear of the unknown: One fear to rule them all? *Journal of Anxiety Disorders* 41 (1), 5–21.

Chandrasekhar, S. (2010): Beauty and the quest for beauty in science. *Physics Today* 63, 57–62.

Chatterjee, A. K. (2014): *The Aesthetic Brain: How We Evolved to Desire Beauty and Enjoy Art.* New York: Oxford University Press.

Cherniwchan, C., Ghassemi, A., Keating, J. (2013): *Mathematical ethnographies: Is a mathematical proof beautiful?* [Online] Retrieved [2018-10-10] from: <https://www.youtube.com/watch?v=tANB6hXmY7U>.

Cornelissen, P. L., Toveé, M. J., Bateson, M. (2009): Patterns of subcutaneous fat deposition and the relationship between body mass index and waist-to-hip ratio: Implications for models of physical attractiveness. *Journal of Theoretical Biology* 256 (3), 343–350.

Cortel, G. W., Hsiao, J. H. (2011): Neurocomputational Models of Face Processing. In: Calder, A. J., Rhodes, G., Johnson, M. H., Haxby, J. V. (eds.): *The Oxford Handbook of Face Perception.* Oxford: Oxford University Press, 401–423.

Costreie, V. S. (2012): What could mathematical cognition tell us about the actual world. *Procedia - Social and Behavioral Sciences* 33, 138–142.

Cowie, R. (2014): Beauty Is Felt, Not Calculated; and It Does Not Fit in Boxes. In: Schellekens, E., Goldie, P. (eds.): *The Aesthetic Mind.* Oxford: Oxford University Press, 89–105.

Damasio, A. (1994): *Descartes' Error: Emotion, Reason, and the Human Brain.* New York: G. P. Putnam Publishing.

Démuth, A. (2005): *Čo je to farba?* Bratislava: Iris.

Démuth, A. (2009a): Intuícia ako výpočet so zastretým algoritmom riešenia? In: Krámský, D. (ed.): *Kognintivní věda dnes a zítra.* Liberec: Bor, 81–86.

Démuth, A. (2009b): *Poznanie, vedenie alebo interpretácia?* Pusté Úľany: Schola Philosophica.

Démuth, A. (2013a): *Perception Theories.* Krakow: Towarzystwo Słowaków w Polsce.

Démuth, A. (2013b): *Philosophical Aspects of the History of Science*. Krakow: Towarzystwo Słowaków w Polsce.

Démuth, A. (2016): Tri historické matematické prístupy ku skúmaniu krásy. *Filozofia* 71 (9), 759–770.

Démuthová, S., Démuth, A. (2016): The role of intelligence in female face perception: Verbal not visual-spatial IQ intervenes with intelligence assessment in face composites. In: *Sixth Global Academic Meeting* (GAM 2016), 01-02 November, Dubai, UAE: Proceedings. Kocani: European Scientific Institute (ESI), 62–73.

Démuth, A. (2019a): *Beauty, Aesthetic Experience and Emotional Affective States*. Berlin: Peter Lang Verlag.

Démuth, A. (2019b): What Is Music and What Function Does It Serve in Our Lives? Three Forms of Synchronicity. In: Démuth, A. (ed.): *Cognitive Aspects of Aesthetic Experience - Selected Problems*. Berlin: Peter Lang Verlag, 107–132.

Démuth, A. Démuthová, S. (2018): Intelligence attracts. *The International Journal of Arts & Sciences* 11 (1), 145–156.

Démuth, A., Démuthová, S. (2019): The Comparison as the Standardization of Aesthetic Norms. In: Babich, B. (ed.): *Reading David Hume's "Of The Standard of Taste"*. Berlin: De Gruyter, 249–261.

Démuth, A., Rušinová, M. (2019): *Cognitive Aesthetics in Classical German Philosophy*. Berlin: Peter Lang Verlag.

Démuthová, S., Selecká, L., Démuth, A. (2019): *Human Facial Attractiveness in Psychological Research (an Evolutionary Approach)*. Berlin: Peter Lang Verlag.

Devlin, K. (2000): *Do Mathematicians Have Different Brains? The Math Gene: How Mathematical Thinking Evolved and Why Numbers Are Like Gossip*. New York: Basic Books.

Dio, C. D., Macaluso, E., Rizzolatti, G. (2007): The golden beauty: Brain response to classical and renaissance sculptures. *PLoS One 2 (11): e1201, 1–9.*

Dion, K., Berscheid, E., Walster, E. (1972): What is beautiful is good. *Journal of Personality and Social Psychology* 24 (3), 285–290.

Douchová, V. (2016): Birkhoff's aesthetic measure. *Acta Universitatis Carolinae. Philosophica et historica* 2015 (1), 39–53.

Drummond, J. (2009): Feelings, emotions, and truly perceiving the valuable. *The Modern Schoolman* 86, 363–379.

Dutton, D. (2010): *The Art Instinct: Beauty, Pleasure, & Human Evolution*. Oxford: Oxford University Press.

Easton, G. (2004): Future face. *British Medical Journal,* 329 (7470), 863.

Eastwick, P. W., Finkel, E. J. (2008): Sex differences in mate preferences revisited: Do people know what they initially desire in a romantic partner? *Journal of Personality and Social Psychology* 94 (2), 245–264.

Eastwick, P. W., Eagly, A. H., Finkel, E. J., Johnson, S. E. (2011): Implicit and explicit preferences for physical attractiveness in a romantic partner: A double dissociation in predictive validity. *Journal of Personality and Social Psychology* 101 (5), 993–1011.

Eco, U. (ed.) (2005): *Dějiny krásy*. Praha: Argo.

Eisenthal, Y., Dror, G., Ruppin, E. (2006): Facial attractiveness: Beauty and the machine. *Neural Computation* 18 (1), 119–142.

Elgammal, A., Sahel, B. (2015): Quantifying Creativity in Art Networks. In: Toivonen, H., Colton, S., Cook, M., & Ventura, D. (eds): *Proceedings of the Sixth International Conference on Computational Creativity* (ICCC 2015), June 29–July 2, 2015, Park City, UT, USA, Provo: Brigham Young University, 9–46.

Engler, G. (1990): Aesthetics in science and in art, *British Journal of Aesthetics* 30, 24–34.

Enquist, M., Arak, A. (1994): Symmetry, beauty and evolution. *Nature* 372, 169–172.

Etcoff, N. (1999): *Survival of the Prettiest: The Science of Beauty*. New York: Anchor Books.

Feingold, A. (1988): Matching for attractiveness in romantic partners and same-sex friends: A meta-analysis and theoretical critique. *Psychological Bulletin* 104 (2), 226–235.

Fink, B., Neave, N., Manning, J. T., Grammer, K. (2006): Facial symmetry and judgements of attractiveness, health and personality. *Personality and Individual Differences,* 41 (3), 491–499.

Fisher, M. L., Voracek, M. (2006): The shape of beauty: Determinants of female physical attractiveness. *Journal of Cosmetic Dermatology* 5 (2), 190–194.

Flyn, C. (2017): What makes maths beautiful? New Humanist. [Online] Retrieved [2018-07-07] from: <https://newhumanist.org.uk/articles/5208/what-makes-maths-beautiful>.

Francis, M. S. J. (2013): *The criminal subject: Alphonse Bertillon and Francis Galton, their aesthetics and their legacies.* PhD thesis, University of Nottingham. [Online] Retrieved [2018-07-06] from: <http://eprints.nottingham.ac.uk/13349/1/TCS_LR.pdf>.

Freedman, R. E., Carter, M. M., Sbrocco, T., Gray, J. J. (2004): Ethnic differences in preferences for female weight and waist-to-hip ratio: A comparison of African-American and White American college and community samples. *Eating Behaviors* 5 (3), 191–198.

Freedman, R. E., Carter, M. M., Sbrocco, T., Gray, J. J. (2007): Do men hold African-American and Caucasian women to different standards of beauty? *Eating Behaviors* 8 (3), 319–333.

Fugere, M. (2017): Why physical attraction matters, and when it might not. *Psychology Today*. (05/01/2017). [Online] Retrieved [2018-10-10] from: <https://www.psychologytoday.com/us/blog/dating-and-mating/201701/why-physical-attraction-matters-and-when-it-might-not>.

Fugère, M. A., Cousins, A. J., Maclaren, S. (2015): (Mis)matching in physical attractiveness and women's resistance to mate guarding. *Personality and Individual Differences* 87, 190–195.

Garnier, R., Taylor, J. (1996): *100% Mathematical Proof.* New York: John Wiley & Sons, 1996.

Ghyka, M. (1946): *The Geometry of Art and Life.* New York: Sheed and Ward.

Glynn, I. (2010): *Elegance in Science. The Beauty of Simplicity.* New York: Oxford University Press.

Griffin, A. M., Langlois, J. H. (2006): Stereotype directionality and attractiveness stereotyping: Is beauty good or is ugly bad? *Social Cognition* 24 (2), 187–206.

Hadot, P. (2004): *What is Ancient Philosophy?* Cambridge: Belknap Press; An Imprint of Harvard University Press.

Hägerhäll, C. M., Ode Sang, Å., Englund, J. E., Ahlner, F., Rybka, K., Huber, J., Burenhult, N. (2018): Do humans really prefer semi-open natural landscapes? A cross-cultural reappraisal. *Frontiers in Psychology* 9, 822.

Haran, B. (2012): *Brown's criterion. And a nice number trick.* [Online] Retrieved [2018-12-06] from: A lecture by James Grime. <https://youtu.be/kQZmZRE0cQY>. In: Numberphile. Videos about numbers. <http://www.numberphile.com/>.

Hardy, G. H. (1940): *A Mathematician's Apology.* Cambridge: Cambridge University Press.

Harper, D. (2018a): "Attract" in: *Online Etymology Dictionary.* [Online] Retrieved [2018-11-21] from: <https://www.etymonline.com/word/attract#etymonline_v_18917>.

Harper, D. (2018b): "Symmetry" in: *Online Etymology Dictionary.* [Online] Retrieved [2018-11-21] <https://www.etymonline.com/word/symmetry >.

Heidegger, M. (1995): *Bytí a čas.* Praha: Oikoymenh.

Herz-Fischler, R. (2004): *Adolph Zeising, 1810–1876: The Life and Work of a German Intellectual.* Ottawa: Mzinhigan Publications.

Hockenberry, J., Spiropulu, M., Lightman, A., Gross, D., Dijkgraaf, R. (2016): *Beyond beauty: The predictive power of symmetry.* [Online] Retrieved [2018-10-21] from: <https://www.worldsciencefestival.com/videos/beyond-beauty-the-predictive-power-of-symmetry/>.

Hoenig, F. (2005): Defining computational aesthetics. In: *Computationalaesthetics'05 proceedings of the first eurographics conference oncomputational aesthetics in graphics, visualization and imaging.* Girona: Eurographics Association, 13–18.

Hofstadter, D. (1979): *Gödel, Escher, Bach: An Eternal Golden Braid.* New York: Basic Books.

Hofstadter, D. (2007): *I Am a Strange Loop.* New York: Basic Books.

Hogenboom, E. (2016): *What is the most beautiful equation?* BBC Earth (20.1.2016) [Online] Retrieved [2018-10-21] from: <http://www.bbc.com/earth/story/20160120-you-decide-what-is-the-most-beautiful-equation-ever-written>.

Hope, D., Bates, T., Penke, L., Gow, A. J., Starr J. M., Deary, I. J. (2013): Symmetry of the face in old age reflects childhood social status. *Economics & Human Biology* 11 (2), 236–244.

Hoss, R. A., Ramsey, J. L., Griffin, A. M., Langlois, J. H. (2005): The role of facial attractiveness and facial masculinity/femininity in sex classification of faces. *Perception* 34 (12), 1459–1474.

Huffman, C. (2016): "Pythagoreanism". In: Zalta, E. N. (ed.): *The Stanford Encyclopedia of Philosophy* (Winter 2016 Edition), [Online] Retrieved [2018-09-09] from: <https://plato.stanford.edu/archives/win2016/entries/pythagoreanism/>.

Hume, D. (2008): Of the Standard of Taste. In: Copley, S., Edgar. A. (eds.): *David Hume: Selected Essays.* Oxford: Oxford University Press, 133–153.

Hungerford, M. W. (1890): *Molly Bawn.* London: Smith, Elder & Company.

Hunt, M. (2007): *The Story of Psychology.* Updated and revised edition. New York, Toronto: Anchor Books.

Inglis, M., Aberdein, A. (2014): Beauty is not simplicity: An analysis of mathematicians' proof appraisals. *Philosophia Mathematica* (III) 23 (1), 87–109.

Ishizu, T., Zeki, S. (2011): Toward a brain-based theory of beauty. *PLoS One* 6 (7), e21852.

Johnson, S. J. B., Steinerberger, S. (2019): Intuitions about mathematical beauty: A case study in the aesthetic experience of ideas. *Cognition.* 189 (8), 242–259.

Johnstone, R. A. (1994): Female preference for symmetrical males as a by-product of selection for mate recognition. *Nature* 372, 172–175.

Jones, P. (2011): Hume on the Arts and "The Standard of Taste": Texts and Contexts. In: Norton, D. F., Taylor, J. (eds.): *The Cambridge Companion to Hume.* Second edition. Cambridge: Cambridge University Press, 414–446.

Kahneman, D. (2011): *Thinking, Fast and Slow.* London: Penguin Books.

Kant, I. (1977): *Kritik der reinen Vernunf.* 2. Auflage. Frankfurt am Main: Suhrkamp.

Kant, I. (1975): *Kritika soudnosti.* Praha: Odeon.

Karamanides, D. (2006): *Pythagoras: Pioneering Mathematician and Musical Theorist of Ancient Greece.* New York: The Rosen Publishing Group.

Kawabata, H., Zeki, S. (2004): Neural correlates of beauty. *Journal of Neurophysiology* 91 (4), 1699–1705.

Keating, C. F., Mazur, A., Segall, M. H. (1981): A cross-cultural exploration of physiognomic traits of dominance and happiness. *Ethology and Sociobiology* 2 (1), 41–48.

Kessler, V. (2018): God becomes beautiful ... in mathematics. *HTS Teologiese Studies/Theological Studies* 74 (1), e1–e7.

Kissak, P. F. (ed.) (2016): *Symmetry Breaking & Symmetry in Cosmology: The Fundamentals of The Cosmological Timeline.* Scotts Valley: CreateSpace Independent Publishing Platform.

Kleisner, K., Chvátalová, V., Flegr, J. (2014): Perceived intelligence is associated with measured intelligence in men but not women. *PLoS One* 9(3), e81237, 1–7.

Kobayashi, M. (2018): Makoto Kobayashi – Facts. NobelPrize.org. Nobel Media AB 2018. [Online] Retrieved [2018-11-22] from: <https://www.nobelprize.org/prizes/physics/2008/kobayashi/facts/>.

Kuhn, T. S. (1996): *The Structure of Scientific Revolutions.* Third edition. Chicago: University of Chicago Press.

Kurzban, R., Weeden, J. (2005): HurryDate: Mate preferences in action. *Evolution and Human Behavior* 26 (3), 227–244.

Kusugal, P., Ruttonji, Z., Gowda, R., Rajpurohit, L., Lad, P., Ritu (2015): Three-dimensional facial analyses of Indian and Malaysian women. *Contemporary Clinical Dentistry* 6 (3), 332–336.

Kvasz, L. (1997): Dejiny náboženstva a matematika. In: *Hieron. Religionistická ročenka II.* Bratislava: SSŠN a Chronos, 115–129.

Kvasz, L. (2010): Vedecká racionalita a súčasné prístupy k transcendencii. In: Slavkovský, R. A., Vydrová, J., Vydra, A. (eds.): *Boh a racionalita.* Pusté Úľany: Schola Philosophica, 213–232.

Land, E. H. (1983): Recent advances in retinex theory and some implications for cortical computations: Color vision and the natural image. *Proceedings of the National Academy of Sciences USA* 80, 5163–5169.

Land, E. H., Hubel, D. H., Livingstone, M. S., Perry, S. H., Burns, M. M. (1983): Colour-generating interactions across the corpus callosum. *Nature* 303 (16 June) 616–618.

Langlois, J. H., Roggman, L. A. (1990): Attractive faces are only average. *Psychological Science* 1 (2), 115–121.

Leibniz, G. W. (1714): The Principles of Nature and of Grace based on Reason. In: Leroy E. Loemker (ed.) (1970): *Philosophical Papers and Letters.* Dordrecht: Reidel.

Leibniz, G. W. (1690–1698a): On Felicity. In: Patrick Riley (ed.): *The Political Writings of Leibniz.* Cambridge: Cambridge University Press, 1972.

Leibniz, G. W. (1690–1698b): On Wisdom. In: Leroy E. Loemker *(ed.): Philosophical Papers and Letters.* Dordrecht: Reidel, 1970.

Levin, E. I. (1978): Dental esthetics and the golden proportion. *The Journal of Prosthetic Dentistry* 40, 244–252.

Levy-Eichel, M. (2018): Mathematics as thought. In: *Aeon (digital magazine).* [Online] Retrieved [2018-12-10] from: <https://aeon.co/essays/the-secret-intellectual-history-of-mathematics>.

Li, N. P., Valentine, K. A., Patel, L. (2011): Mate preferences in the US and Singapore: A cross-cultural test of the mate preference priority model. *Personality and Individual Differences* 50 (2), 291–294.

Liang, X., Zebrowitz, L. A., Zhang, Y. (2010): Neural activation in the "reward circuit" shows a nonlinear response to facial attractiveness. *Social Neuroscience* 5 (3), 320–334.

Lippa, R. A. (2007): The preferred traits of mates in a cross-national study of heterosexual and homosexual men and women: An examination of biological and cultural influences. *Archives of Sexual Behavior* 36 (2), 193–208.

Little, A. C., Jones, B. C. (2003): Evidence against perceptual bias views for symmetry preferences in human faces. *Proceedings of the Royal Society of London Series B – Biological Science* 270, 1759–1763.

Little, A. C., Perrett, D. I. (2007): Using composite images to assess accuracy in personality attribution to faces. *British Journal of Psychology* 98 (1), 111–126.

Loomis, E. S. (1968): *The Pythagorean Proposition. Its Demonstration Analyzed and Classified and Bibliography of Sources for Data of the Four Kinds of 'Proofs'.* Washington: National Council of Teachers of Mathematics.

Luo, S., Zhang, G. (2009): What leads to romantic attraction: Similarity, reciprocity, security, or beauty? Evidence from a speed-dating study. *Journal of Personality* 77 (4), 933–964.

Lutoslawska, G., Malara, M., Tomaszewski, P., Mazurek, K., Czajkowska, A., Kęska, A., Tkaczyk, J. (2014): Relationship between the percentage of body fat and surrogate indices of fatness in male and female Polish active and sedentary students. *Journal of Physiological Anthropology* 13 (33), 10.

Macpherson, F. (2012): Cognitive penetration of colour experience: rethinking the issue in light of an indirect mechanism. *Philosophy and Phenomenological Research*, 84 (1), 24–62.

Mainzer, K. (2005): *Symmetry and Complexity: The Spirit and Beauty of Nonlinear Science.* New Jersey: World Scientific Publishing.

Mantelakis, A., Iosifidis, M., Al-Bitar, Z. B., Antoniadis, V., Wertheim, D., Garagiola, U. (2018): Proportions of the aesthetic African Caribbean face: Idealized ratios, comparison with the golden proportion and perceptions of attractiveness. *Maxillofacial Plastic and Reconstructive Surgery* 40, (20). [Online] Retrieved [2018-12-09] from: <https://doi.org/10.1186/s40902-018-0161-5>.

Maskava, T. (2018): Toshihide Maskawa – Facts. NobelPrize.org. Nobel Media AB 2018. [Online] Retrieved [2018-11-04] from: <https://www.nobelprize.org/prizes/physics/2008/maskawa/facts/>.

Mcallister, J. W. (2005): Mathematical Beauty and the Evolution of the Standards of Mathematical Proof. In: Emmer, M. (ed.): *The Visual Mind II,* Cambridge: MIT Press, 15–34.

Mo C, Xia T, Qin K, Mo L. (2016): Natural tendency towards beauty in humans: Evidence from binocular rivalry. *PLoS One* 11 (3), e0150147.

Montoya, R. (2008): I'm hot, so I'd say you're not: The influence of objective physical attractiveness on mate selection. *Personality and Social Psychology Bulletin* 34 (10), 1315–1331.

Naini, F. H., Moss, J. P., Gill, D. S. (2006): The enigma of facial beauty: Esthetics, proportions, deformity, and controversy. *American Journal of Orthodontics and Dentofacial Orthopedics* 130 (3), 277–282.

Nake, F. (2012): Information aesthetics: An heroic experiment. *Journal of Mathematics and the Arts* 6 (2–3), 65–75.

Nambu, Y. (2018): Yoichiro Nambu – Facts. NobelPrize.org. Nobel Media AB 2018. Online [2018-11-22], Retrieved from: <https://www.nobelprize.org/prizes/physics/2008/nambu/facts/>.

O`Toole, A. J. (2011): Cognitive and Computional Approaches to Face Recognition. In: Calder, A. J., Rhodes, G., Johnson, M. H., Haxby, J. V. (eds.): *The Oxford Handbook of Face Perception.* Oxford: Oxford University Press, 15–30.

Pallett, P. M., Link, S., Lee, K. (2010): New "golden" ratios for facial beauty. *Vision Research* 50 (2), 149–154.

Penrose, R., Shimony, A., Cartwright, N., Hawking, S. (1997): *The Large, the Small and the Human Mind.* Cambridge: Cambridge University Press.

Penton-Voak, I. S., Pound, N., Little, A. C., Perrett, D. I. (2006): Personality judgements from natural and composite facial images: More evidence for a "kernel of truth" in social perception. *Social Cognition* 24 (5), 607–640.

Perilloux, C., Fleischman, D. S., Buss, D. M. (2011): Meet the parents: Parent-offspring convergence and divergence in mate preferences. *Personality and Individual Differences* 50 (2), 253–258.

Perrett, D. (2010): *In Your Face. The New Science of Human Attraction.* London: Palgrave McMillan.

Perrett, D. I., May, K. A, Yoshikawa, S. (1994): Facial shape and judgements of female attractiveness. *Nature,* 368 (6468), 239–242.

Petkovsky, O. (2016): The searching for a proportional system of the human body for students of the art school in Slovakia, *International Journal of Arts and Commerce* 5 (4), 20–29.

Pogue, D. (2018): Is Art Created by AI Really Art? *Scientific American* (February 1). [Online] Retrieved [2018-05-05] from: <https://www.scientificamerican.com/article/is-art-created-by-ai-really-art/?redirect=1>. Available also: Pogue, D. (2018): "The Robotic Artist Problem". *Scientific American* 318, 2, 23 (February 2018) doi:10.1038/scientificamerican0218-23.

Popper, K. R. (1984): *In Search of a Better World. Lectures & Essays from Thirty Years.* London: Routledge.

Prokopakis, E. P., Vlastos, I. M., Picavet, V., Trenité, G. N., Thomas, R., Cingi, C., Hellings, P. W. (2013): The golden ratio in facial symmetry. *Rhinology* 51 (1), 18–21.

Raskin, J. (1998): Effectiveness of mathematics. A reply to Eugene Wigner's paper, "The unreasonable effectiveness of mathematics in the Natural Sciences" and Hamming's essay "The unreasonable effectiveness of mathematics." [Online] Retrieved [2018-12-01] from: <https://spacetimecentre.org/vpetkov/courses/effectiveness_mathematics.html>.

Reid, T. (1969): *Essays on the Intellectual Powers of Man.* Cambridge: MIT Press.

Reutskaja, E., Lindner, A., Nagel, R., Andersen, R. A., Camerer, C. F. (2018): Choice overload reduces neural signatures of choice set value in dorsal striatum and anterior cingulate cortex. *Nature Human Behaviour.* [Online] Retrieved [2018-11-30] from: <http://resolver.caltech.edu/CaltechAUTHORS:20181001-113521255>.

Rhodes, G. (2006): The evolutionary psychology of facial beauty. *Annual Review of Psychology* 57, 199–226.

Rhodes, G., Sumich, A., Byatt, G. (1999): Are average facial configuration attractive only because of their symmetry? *Psychological Science* 10, 52–58.

Rhodes, G., Yoshikawa, S., Clark, A., Lee, K., Mckay, R., Akamatsu, S. (2001): Attractiveness of facial averageness and symmetry in non-Western cultures: In search of biologically based standards of beauty. *Perception* 30 (5), 611–625.

Ridley, M. (1993): *The Red Queen: Sex and the Evolution of Human Nature.* New York: Harper Perennial.

Rigau, J., Feixas, M., Sbert, M. (2008): Informational aesthetics measures. *Computational Aesthetics* March, 24–34.

Rolls, E. T. (2014): The Origins of Aesthetics. In: Schellekens, E., Goldie P. (eds.): *The Aesthetic Mind.* Oxford: Oxford University Press, 116–165.

Rookes, P., Willson, J. (2000): *Perception: Theory, Development and Organisation.* London, Philadelphia: Routledge.

Rossetti, A., De Menezes, M., Rosati, R., Ferrario, V. F., Sforza, C. (2013): The role of the golden proportion in the evaluation of facial esthetics. *The Angle Orthodontist* 83 (5), 801–808.

Russell, B. (1917): The Study of Mathematics. In: *Mysticism and Logic: And Other Essays.* London: Longman, 58–73. Online [2018-10-11] Retrieved from: <https://en.wikisource.org/wiki/Mysticism_and_Logic_and_Other_Essays>.

Sacks, O., Wasserman, R. (1987): The case of the colorblind painter. *The New York Review of Books.* 1-18. (19 November 1987). [Online] Retrieved [2018-07-07] from: <https://www.csh.rit.edu/~oguns/school/psychology/Articles/colorblindpainter.pdf>.

Salimpoor, V. N., Benovoy, M., Larcher, K., Dagher, A., Zatorre, R. J. (2011): Anatomically distinct dopamine release during anticipation and experience of peak emotion to music. *Nature Neuroscience* 14 (2), 257–262.

Satyam, V. R. (2016): The importance of surprise in mathematical beauty, *Journal of Humanistic Mathematics* 6 (1), 196–210.

Scha, R., Bod, R. (1993): Computationele esthetica. *Informatie en Informatiebeleid* 11, 1, 54–63. Schmidhuber, J. (2009): Simple algorithmic theory of subjective beauty, novelty, surprise, interestingness, attention, curiosity, creativity, art, science, music, jokes. *Journal of SICE* 48 (1), 21–32.

Schmidhuber, J. (1991): Curious model-building control systems. *International Joint Conference on Neural Networks,* Singapore, 2, 1458–1463. IEEE Press.

Schmidhuber, J. (1997): Low-complexity art. *Leonardo* 30 (2), 97–103.

Schwartz, B. (2004): *The Paradox of Choice – Why More Is Less.* New York: Harper Perennial.

Scott, I. M., Pound, N., Stephen, I. D., Clark, A. P., Ian, S., Penton-Voak, I. S. (2010): Does masculinity matter? The contribution of masculine face shape to male attractiveness in humans. *PLoS One* 5 (10), e13585, 1–10.

Selecká, L. (2017): How women make their choices: Personal characteristics in relation to dominant/submissive or extrovert/introvert men face preference. In: Arslan, H., Icbay, M. A., Tomescu, M. (eds.), *Communication and Digital Media.* Bialystok: E-BWN, 283–292.

Shaffer, D. R., Crepaz, N., Sun, C. (2000): Physical attractiveness stereotyping in cross-cultural perspective: Similarities and differences between Americans and Taiwanese. *Journal of Cross-Cultural Psychology* 31(5), 557–582.

Sharot, T., Shiner, T., Brown, A. C., Fan, J., Dolan, R. J. (2009): Dopamine enhances expectation of pleasure in humans. *Current Biology* 19 (24), 2077–2080.

Shell, T. L., Woods, M. G. (2004): Facial aesthetics and the divine proportion: A comparison of surgical and non-surgical class II treatment. *Australian Orthodontic Journal* 20 (2), 51–63.

Shen, H., Chau, D. K., Su, J., Zeng, L. L., Jiang, W., He, J., Fan, J., Hu, D. (2016): Brain responses to facial attractiveness induced by facial proportions: Evidence from an fMRI study. *Scientific Reports* 6, 35905.

Simpson, D. (2005): Phrenology and the neurosciences: contributions of F. J. Gall and J. G. Spurzheim. *ANZ Journal of Surgery* 75 (6), 475–482.

Sinclair, N. (2004): The roles of the aesthetic in mathematical inquiry. *Mathematical Thinking and Learning* 6 (3), 261–284.

Sinclair, N. (2006): *Mathematics and Beauty.* New York: Teachers College Press, 2006.

Sinclair, N. (2008): Attending to the aesthetic in the mathematics classroom, *For the Learning of Mathematics 28 (1), 29–35.*

Singh, D. (1993a): Adaptive significance of female physical attractiveness: Role of waist-to-hip ratio. *Journal of Personality and Social Psychology* 65 (2), 293–307.

Singh, D. (1993b): Body shape and women's attractiveness. The critical role of waist-to-hip ratio *Human Nature* 4 (3), 297–321.

Singh, D., Young, R. K. (2001): Body weight, waist-to-hip ratio, breasts, and hips: Role in judgments of female attractiveness and desirability for relationships. *Ethology and Sociobiology* 16 (6), 483–507.

Slavkovský, A. (2017): The Beauty of Mathematics and the Mathematics of Beauty. In: Démuth A. (ed.): *The Cognitive Aspects of Aesthetic Experience – Introduction.* Frankfurt am Main: Peter Lang Verlag, 141–161.

Sprecher, S. (1989): The importance to males and females of physical attractiveness, earning potential, and expressiveness in initial attraction. *Sex Roles* 21 (9–10), 591–607.

Stipp, D. (2017): *A Most Elegant Equation: Eulers Formula and the Beauty of Mathematics.* New York: Basic Books.

Symons, D. (1979): *The Evolution of Human Sexuality.* New York: Oxford University Press.

Symons, D. (1995): Beauty Is in the Adaptations of the Beholder: The Evolutionary Psychology of Human Female Sexual Attractiveness. In: Abramson, P. R., Pinkerton, S. D. (eds.): *Sexual Nature/Sexual Culture.* Chicago: The University of Chicago Press, 80–120.

Šmajs, J. (1990): *Příroda a kultura.* Praha: Nakladatelství Svoboda.

Tappenden, J. (2008): Mathematical Concepts and Definitions. In: Mancosu, P. (ed.): *The Philosophy of Mathematical Practice.* Oxford: Oxford University Press, 256–275.

Teicher, M. (2012): The Mathematics of Beauty. *IAS The Institute Letter* Fall 2012. [Online] Retrieved [2018-12-08] from: <https://www.ias.edu/ideas/2012/teicher-mathematics-beauty>.

Thao, H., Overbeek, G., Engels, R. E. (2010): Effects of attractiveness and social status on dating desire in heterosexual adolescents: An experimental study. *Archives of Sexual Behavior* 39 (5), 1063–1071.

Tik, M., Sladky, R., Di Bernardi Luft, C., Willinger, D., Hoffmann, A., Banissy, M. J., Bhattacharya, J., Windischberger, C. (2018): Ultra-high-field fMRI insights on insight: Neural correlates of the Aha!-moment. *Human Brain Mapping* 39 (8), 3241–3252.

Todorov, A. (2008): Evaluating faces on trustworthiness: An extension of systems for recognition of emotions signaling approach/avoidance behaviors. *Annals of the New York Academy of Sciences*, 1124, 208–224.

Tonelli, F. (2013): Science as ground of the Renaissance artists. Clinical cases in mineral and bone metabolism. *The Official Journal of the Italian Society of Osteoporosis, Mineral Metabolism, and Skeletal Diseases* 10 (1), 68–69.

Tremearne, A. J. N. (1914): A new head-measurer. *Man* 15, 87–88.

Tsukiura, T., Cabeza, R. (2011): Shared brain activity for aesthetic and moral judgments: Implications for the beauty-is-good stereotype, *Social Cognitive an Affective Neuroscience* 6 (1), 138–148.

Valentine, J. W. (2014): "Bilateria" in: *McGraf-Hill Acces Science. Encyclopedia of Science & Technology Online.* [Online] Retrieved [2018-11-11] from: <https://web.archive.org/web/20080118213208/http://www.accessscience.com/abstract.aspx?id=802620&referURL=http%3A%2F%2Fwww.accessscience.com%2Fcontent.aspx%3Fid%3D802620>.

Vopěnka, P. (2001): *Úhelný kámen evropské vzdělanosti a moci.* Praha: Práh.

Wang, G., Djafarian, K., Egedigwe, C. A., El Hamdouchi, A., Ojiambo, R., Ramuth, H., Wallner-Liebmann, S. J., Lackner, S., Diouf, A., Sauciuvenaite, J., Hambly, C., Vaanholt, L. M., Faries, M. D., Speakman, J. R. (2015): The relationship of female physical attractiveness to body fatness. *PeerJ.* 3, e1155.

Warren, M. (2019): Even People Without Mathematical Training Experience The "Beauty" Of Maths. *The British Psychological Society. Research Digest.* (23. May 2019). [Online] Retrieved [12.7.2019] from <https://digest.bps.org.uk/2019/05/23/even-people-without-mathematical-training-experience-the-beauty-of-maths>.

Weeden, J., Sabini, J. (2005): Physical attractiveness and health in Western societies: A review. *Psychological Bulletin* 131 (5), 635–653.

Wells, D. (1990): Are these the most beautiful? *The Mathematical Intelligencer* 12 (3), 37–41.

Westra, A. (2010): Gödel, Hofstadter, & the Self: A Critical Review of Douglas Hofstadter's I Am a Strange Loop. *Numéro Cinq* (online journal), 1 (6), [Online] Retrieved [2018-12-08] from: <http://numerocinqmagazine.com/2010/07/01/godel-hofstadter-the-self-an-essay-by-adam-westra/>.

Wigner, E. P. (1960): The Unreasonable Effectiveness of Mathematics in the Natural Sciences. *Communications in Pure and Applied Mathematics,* 13 (I) (February 1960). New York: John Wiley & Sons, Inc.

Wilson, G. D., Brazendale, A. H. (1974): Psychological correlates of sexual attractiveness: An empirical demonstration of denial and fantasy gratification phenomena? *Social Behavior and Personality: An International Journal* 2, 30–34.

Winston, J. S., O'Doherty, J., Kilner, J. M., Perrett, D. I., Dolan, R. J. (2007): Brain systems for assessing facial attractiveness. *Neuropsychologia* 45, 195–206.

Zebrowitz, L. A., Wang, R., Bronstad, P., Eisenberg, D., Undurraga, E., Reyes-García, V., Godoy, R. (2012): First impressions from faces among U.S. and culturally isolated Tsimane' people in the Bolivian rainforest. *Journal of Cross-Cultural Psychology* 43 (1), 119–134.

Zeki, S., Chén, O. Y., Romaya, J. P. (2018): The biological basis of mathematical beauty. *Frontiers in Human Neuroscience*, 12, 467 (30 Nov). [Online] Retrieved [2018-11-30] from: <https://doi.org/10.3389/fnhum.2018.00467>.

Zeki, S., Romaya, J. P., Benincasa, D., Atiyah, M. T., Michael. F. (2014): The experience of mathematical beauty and its neural correlates. *Frontiers in Human Neuroscience.* 8, 68. (13 Feb). [Online] Retrieved [2018-11-09] from: <https://doi.org/10.3389/fnhum.2014.00068>.

8. About Authors

Andrej Démuth was born in Bratislava, Slovakia, in 1974. After a graduate degree in philosophy (1997) and psychology (2000) and a doctorate in systematic philosophy (2000), studied at Trnava University, Trnava, he was an Assistant Professor in the Department of Philosophy, Trnava University (2000–2009) and the University of Ss. Cyril and Methodius, Trnava (2006–2010) and Associate Professor at Trnava University (2009–2014).
He was the Professor and Head of the Department of Philosophy at Trnava University (since 2009 till 2019) and since 2018 he is the Professor of Philosophy at Comenius University, Bratislava. He is the author of several books *Homo – anima cognoscens* (Iris 2003), *Čo je to farba?* [What is colour?] (Iris 2005), *Poznanie, vedenie alebo interpretácia?* [Knowledge, cognition or an interpretation?] (Schola Philosophica 2009, updated version 2013), *Perception Theories* (Towarzystwo Słowaków w Polsce 2013), *Game Theory and the Problem of Decision-Making* (Towarzystwo Słowaków w Polsce 2013), *Philosophical Aspects of the History of Science* (Towarzystwo Słowaków w Polsce 2013), *Introduction to the Study of the History of Epistemology* (Peter Lang Verlag, 2015), *Prolegomena to the Study of Modern Philosophy* (Peter Lang Verlag, 2015), *Beauty, Aesthetic Experience, and Emotional Affective States* (Peter Lang Verlag, 2019) and many scientific articles focused on modern philosophy and epistemology.
He has given lectures at a number of universities in the Czech Republic, Poland and Slovakia and has also completed several short-term research stays at foreign universities (PPLS Edinburgh, UCD Dublin, LUCS Lund, Tallinn University, Tartu University, The Hebrew University of Jerusalem, Uppsala University and Glasgow University); he has taken part in many international conferences and is a member of several scientific associations and councils. He has been awarded several research grants by the Slovak (VEGA, KEGA, APVV), EU and international institutions; he led the EU project for the preparation of a new MA program in Cognitive Studies, which he supervises; he also established the Center for Cognitive Studies at Trnava University.

Slávka Démuthová was born in 1976 in Martin, Slovakia. She obtained her Master's degree in psychology at the Faculty of Humanities of Trnava University, Trnava. During her studies, she spent a year at the British charity organization, Break (Hunstanton, UK), where she worked as a volunteer with children and adults with mental disabilities. In 2000, she obtained her Master's degree in Psychology (Trnava University, Trnava), in 2007, she was awarded the research qualification, Ph.D. (Trnava University, Trnava) and in 2015, she qualified as an Associate Professor at the Masaryk University in Brno (the Czech Republic).
Since 2000, she has been working as an Assistant Professor at the Department of Psychology of the Faculty of Arts and Sciences, University of Ss. Cyril and Methodius in Trnava – currently as an Associate Professor and the Head of the Department of Psychology. She gives the lectures in the field of developmental psy-

chology and the history of psychology. Her primary areas of interest include the problems of children and youths: *Mladistvý delikvent* [The Juvenile Delinquent] (Schola Philosophica 2006), *Biologické koncepcie kriminality* [Biological Conceptions of Crime] (UCM 2012), *Keď umiera dieťa* [When the Child is Dying] (Schola Philosophica 2010), *Kapitoly z tanatológie* [Chapters from Thanatology] (UCM 2013) and the perception of beautiful faces - in: *Cognitive Aspects of Aesthetic Experience - Introduction* (Peter Lang Verlag 2017), *Cognitive Aspects of Aesthetic Experience - Selected Problems* (Peter Lang Verlag 2019).
In addition to working at the University of Ss. Cyril and Methodius, she has completed several research stays and has been invited to give the lectures at universities abroad: The Lund University, SE (2010); The University of Edinburgh, GB (2011); Trinity College Dublin, IRL (2013); The Hebrew University of Jerusalem, IL (2014); Glasgow University, GB (2015); The Cardinal Wyszyński University in Warsaw, PL (2016); Max-Planck-Institut für empirische Ästhetik (Frankfurt am Main, DE, 2017) or The University of Ljubljana, SLO (2018). Since 2010, she has also been lecturing Thanatology at the Masaryk University, Brno (CZ).

Adrián Slavkovský was born in Košice, Slovakia, in 1963. After a graduate degree in mathematics (1986) at Comenius University, Bratislava and theology (1996) at Palacký University, Olomouc, Czech Republic, and a doctorate in systematic philosophy (2002) at Trnava University, Trnava, he was an Assistant Professor at the Department of Philosophy at Trnava University (2002–2014) and then Head of the Department of Philosophy at Trnava University (2007–2009).
Since 2014, he has been an Associate Professor at the Department of Philosophy at Trnava University. He is the author of several books: *Information in the Context of Philosophy and Cognitive Sciences* (Towarzystwo Słowaków w Polsce 2013), *Rationality and Human Cognition* (Towarzystwo Słowaków w Polsce 2013), *Introduction to Philosophy of Language* (Towarzystwo Słowaków w Polsce 2013, as co-author), *Indian and Chinese Philosophy* (Peter Lang Verlag, 2016), *Religious Studies* (Peter Lang Verlag, 2016) and many scientific articles focused on the limits of rationality, the philosophy of spirituality and the relationship between science and belief.
He has given lectures at universities in the Czech Republic and Slovakia and has also completed several short-term research stays at foreign universities (Geneva and The Bossey Institute, Sheffield, Oxford, Prague, Olomouc, Warsaw, Reykjavík) and has taken part in international conferences and is a member of several scientific associations and councils. He is a member of the editorial team of the open-access journal for humanities, *Ostium* (from 2005 to 2018 he was Editor-in-Chief), and is also a member of the editorial team of the open-access journal *Spirituality Studies*. He was prior provincial of Slovak Dominican province (2009–2017).

FSC
www.fsc.org
MIX
Papier | Fördert
gute Waldnutzung
FSC® C083411

Kolibri 360 GmbH
Ferdinand-Jühlke-Straße 7
99095 Erfurt, Deutschland
produktsicherheit@kolibri360.de